LOMATHINDA

LOMATHINDA
ROSE CHIBAMBO SPEAKS

Timwa Lipenga

First published in Malawi in 2019
by Logos – Open Culture
Lilongwe, Malawi
www.logosmw.org

Copyright © 2015 Timwa Lipenga

All Rights Reserved. No part of this work may be reproduced, photocopied, transmitted, stored in a retrieval system, published, performed in public, adapted, broadcast, or recorded in any form or by any means without the prior permission of the copyright owner, except for brief quotations and other non-commercial uses permitted by current legislation.

Edited by Rachel Etter-Phoya and Mona Hakimi
Typeset by Illana Welman
Cover artwork by Lerato Honde (2019)
Cover design by Tayo Kopfer
Printed and bound by ABC Printers

A CIP record for this book is available from the British Library.

ISBN 978-99960-979-1-1

Contents

Map	I
Foreword	II
Introduction	IV
Prologue: Revisiting memories	1
Chapter 1: Mzimba, the Early Days (1920s–1940s)	5
Chapter 2: Moving into Family Roles (1920–1940s)	13
Chapter 3: The Night Walk (1930s–1940s)	21
Chapter 4: Remembering Recreation (1930s–1940s)	27
Chapter 5: Duties in the Kitchen and Maize Field (1930s and 1940s)	33
Chapter 6: Travelling with Childhood Companions (1930s–1940s)	39
Chapter 7: In Search of Education (1930s–1940s)	49
Chapter 8: From the Classroom to Courtship (1940s)	63
Chapter 9: Wedding Preparations and Marriage (1947)	73
Chapter 10: Moving into Political Spaces (1950s)	83
Chapter 11: Out with the Old, in with the New (1950s)	97
Chapter 12: The Meeting in the Bush and Time in Prison (1959–1960)	107
Chapter 13: The Role of Music and Dance in Politics	125
Chapter 14: The Cabinet Crisis (1964)	135
Chapter 15: Leaving Familiar Spaces (1964–1965)	151
Chapter 16: Life Away from Home (1965–1994)	159
Chapter 17: The Return (1994)	169
Chapter 18: A Place on the Banknote (2012)	177
Chapter 19: Returning to Old Routes	183
Epilogue: The Last Word	199
Glossary	204
Index	214

Map

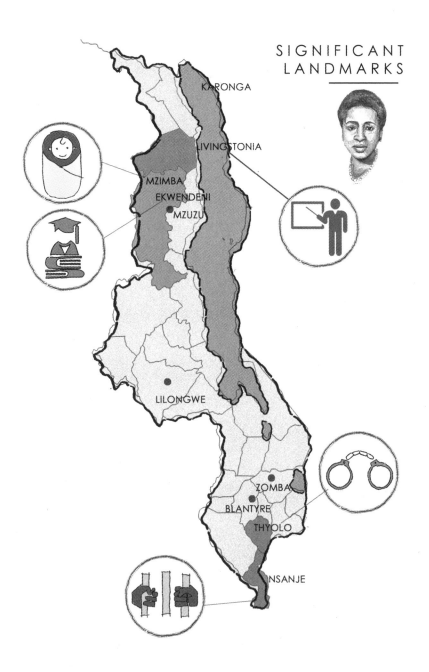

Foreword

"If you know where you came from,
You will know where you are going."

- Rose Lomathinda Chibambo

The history of humankind is the history of men. Men fight wars and decide the fate of nations. Men are heroes; men are discoverers, inventors and leaders. They shape history. Our school books are full of men.

This is how I and many others were taught history at an early age. It seemed women were not part of the story, and when they were, they were often presented in a tragic role. Even today, their voices are mostly unheard and their role in society, politics and history goes largely unaccounted for.

Much later, I learned that history is not a linear and mono-causal development as it appeared in early school books. With a growing interest in politics, I learnt there is not one version of history but many different views, sources and interpretations. Reading biographies of revolutionaries, I was exposed to the influence of dialectics and historical materialism and how economics shape societies, making me better understand the power of ideas and discourse.

But where were the women in history? I finally met them the day I encountered the value of oral history. Thanks to the reportage of contemporary journalism, I understood that history happens every day. I started listening to the voices around me: to the stories of my grandmother and grandfather, of my mother and father, of the people I met around the corner or on far-flung journeys. I finally understood that the past and present are interlinked; all of a sudden, half a century looked like yesterday as it became part of the life of the narrators, people next to me.

Coming five decades after independence, this book provides an insight into the life of Rose Chibambo. It amplifies Chibambo's voice. She tells us the story of her life and how she naturally got involved in politics the moment she sensed the injustice of segregation. It is the story of a woman who stood up and lived up to her convictions, fighting for self-determination, shaping the history of her country, Malawi.

Without any preceding experience in politics but with a natural sense of justice and solidarity, she and her fellow colleagues confronted the ruling system, in colonial times and after independence. The power of women who organise themselves is evident here. For too long, women's contributions to the independence of Africa in general and Malawi in particular have been underestimated. Thanks to Timwa Lipenga, we can now listen to one of their stories.

For an older generation, this book might serve as a reflection about the history and the path Malawi has chosen since independence. For youth, it might serve as an inspiration in the fight for justice and solidarity. It might lead to reflection on how to take part in the future of the country, asking themselves what has become of the ideals of Rose Chibambo and her generation. It is upon them to decide how the future will be shaped, which ideas they will take on and how girls and women can make their voices heard.

Niculin Jäger
Ambassador of Switzerland to Malawi, Zambia and Zimbabwe

Introduction

In November 2011, I was asked by Dr Jessie Kabwila, who was then Head of the English Department at Chancellor College, to lead a project to interview Malawian women. Our aim was to produce and preserve their life stories. The project itself had been suggested by three eminent Malawians in the diaspora: Dr Louis Nthenda and Professors Jack Mapanje and Lupenga Mphande. Dr Nthenda explained that such a project would help to focus on the untold stories of Malawian women in the country's history.

I was happy to take up the project, and together with Dr Kabwila and Dr Hendrina Kachapila-Mazizwa of the History Department (Chancellor College), we drew up a list of the women we would want to interview. This included a wide range: politicians, academics, businesswomen and traditional birth attendants. We gave the self-funded project a name: Malawian Women's Voices Project. We sought women who had engaged in struggles in Malawi in various domains, such as politics, religion, popular culture, education, health and entrepreneurship. We assigned different women to interested researchers.

We wanted to go beyond merely chronicling stories of women to explore how the voices spoke to one another across space and time. We saw the project as a series of dialogues: young speaking with old, dead speaking with living, subaltern speaking with elite, past speaking with present and future.[i]

As we drew up the list, I knew that the woman I wanted to work with was Mrs Rose Chibambo. The more I read about her, the more I was stunned that I had not come across her name, even though I studied Malawian history as an undergraduate. Who was she? What was her role in the 1959 State of Emergency and the 1964 Cabinet Crisis? I met Mrs Chibambo for the first time in 2012. That would be the first of several conversations that year and again in 2013 and 2014. We discussed her role in these pivotal moments in Malawi's history, but she also shared memories of herself as a mischievous adolescent, a pupil in a class dominated by boys, a young woman falling in love and a wife getting involved in politics.

Coming from a background where questions of who does the telling and retelling of history and events are always at the forefront, I decided to avoid narrating Mrs Chibambo's story wherever I could and to let her do the telling. But this was not always possible (this introduction is a case in point). What I have tried to do is to let her tell the story and to keep a section at the end of the 'telling' to make a few additional comments about the context of that particular period. Despite these contextual comments, this is Rose Chibambo's story as she told it to me. The conversations have been structured around the theme of physical and mental journeys because this was what mostly emerged as she told her story. The last chapter ends without any comment from me. There is a reason for this; I want her to have the last word.

Timwa Lipenga, PhD
Department of French
Chancellor College
15 February 2015

Prologue

Revisiting Memories

LOMATHINDA

She is ready to tell her story.

In the telling, there will be pauses: pauses in which she attends to a visitor, takes a sip of water, responds to a telephone call. There will also be longer pauses, spanning months, spanning years.

But there are also pauses in which Rose Chibambo listens to the stranger in her house, the stranger who interrupts by asking questions and giving comments.

It is not just a verbal telling. There are, in the room, images, which are narratives in themselves. Several photographs of her children and grandchildren. A black and white photograph of Rose Chibambo and her late husband, Edwin. The portrait of a fresh-faced Rose which, since 2012, has been on Malawi's two-hundred kwacha note and has earned her the nickname 'K200.'

There is also the picture of Malawi's first cabinet, taken in 1964. She is the only woman in the picture. Later, she will let me take a picture of the picture. In the presence of just one picture, a thousand words must bow in humility. But I still want those thousand words, or more.

There will be plenty of times when the present will interrupt the past, when writing will interrupt speech, when many voices, including mine, will interrupt her narrative. But she is ready to tell her story. Interruptions notwithstanding.

Chapter 1

Mzimba, the Early Days
1920s–1940s

LOMATHINDA

THE EARLY DAYS

I was born Lomathinda Ziba. My father was Aaron Ziba, and my mother was Elizabeth Haraba, Nyaharaba we would say. I was born at Kafukule, on 8th September 1928. My village was called Ephandeni...Ephandeni village, Village Headman Malumbo, Kafukule, in Mzimba.

My father's profession was a teacher. He taught for some years, but at the same time he was a very industrious man. In those early days, shops were too far from our area. He would go and buy stuff such as salt, and he would give it to his nephews to be selling around the village.

After his teaching, when he retired from teaching, he opened up a dairy, and in that dairy he used to make ghee. Ghee sold quite well; it used to be taken to an area near Ekwendeni called Zombwe. Zombwe was a centre where ghee was sold.

But later on, as the years progressed, the government decided that...uhm...dairies should be in a cooperative, they should form a cooperative together with the owners of the milk. He was one of the first people in our area to form that cooperative.

At the same time, he was a very committed Christian. I am told that in his early days, he was one of the people who actually brought the church to our area in Kafukule...the Presbyterian church...the very early days after they had been to Livingstonia—in those days they used to call it Khondowe—where he trained as a teacher.

So he trained at Livingstonia, which was then Khondowe?

It was Khondowe. The main training of those teachers was mostly at Khondowe; it's where teachers were being trained. He was trained from there; even the very early days, they would go to Khondowe and get proper training on how to run the schools.

I was the fifth born of his children. My father first got married and had four children. His wife died. It was then that he married my mother. So I'm the first born to my mother, but I am a fifth born of my father.

Now, about the names you were given. I tried to find out what the second name, Lomathinda, means, and Professor Soko[1] told me that it means 'snatched from the grave,' I think he said. So I'm

---

[1] At the time of the interview, Professor Boston Soko was Professor of French at Mzuzu University, Malawi. He has since retired from the University. He is the author of *Vimbuza the Healing Dance of Malawi* (Mzuzu: Mzuni Press, 2014).

interested in whether you tried to find out why you had been given those names. Why Rose? Why Lomathinda?

My mother told me that my name was given to me by my aunt. The sister of my father. She told me that my birth was a very difficult birth. You know, in the villages, in those days, it used to be very difficult. Because in most cases, when one is in labour, most of the elderly would be there. There would be, really, a number of elders, trying to give instructions, what to do in order to deliver a baby.

So I understand it was really a difficult labour, but it was later on, my aunt chased away everybody in the house. Said, 'You all get out. I'll remain alone. With her.' And it was, when she remained alone, that they did what they did, until I was born. So, when I was born, she said, 'This is Lomathinda.'

And Rose?

Um... (*Laughs.*) E-e-h, the name Rose, I was given by my late husband. (*Laughs.*) I will tell you more when we come to that part.

Okay. But suffice to say that Rose was not the name you were called as a child.

No. No. I grew up as Lomathinda.

And how many children did your father have with your mother?

We were six.

The one that came after me was a boy; he died at the age of fourteen. He had already started Standard Two in those days. And then the one that came after him died at the age of one. She was a girl.

Then the last one died at the age of one. He was also a boy. And this one died actually after my father had died. He died just two years after my father had died. Three of the children died, and there were three of us left. There were three girls who survived, and I was one of them.

Would you remember the causes of death?

In those days, you know, hospitals were very far, and I wouldn't really know what were the causes of death. But in the villages, people talk so much.

Yes, they do.

And I think our family was not very favoured. But my father died after I had married and the last-born boy had already been born. So I was told that he was poisoned.

This boy who died?

No, my father. My father was poisoned. He had been called to have some sweet beer at a certain house. It was on a Saturday. After that, in the evening, he didn't feel quite well.

And then, on Sunday, the whole of his chest had swollen, so much, that I'm told he suffered…so much. And then, on Monday, he died.

So this means it all happened within three days?

It all happened within three days.

So…I guess at the time there must have been some people who were suspected…

Yes, within the village, people were suspected. But the way things were, they had nowhere to go and report to say, 'Ah, he took this,' and that they would take the body to the hospital for a post-mortem. There wasn't such a thing because it was right in the rural area at that time. So they just buried him and the suspicion went on. And the person who was suspected ran away from the village.

And never returned?

Never returned.

Would you remember the name?

I do, but never mind.

Chibambo's Paternal Ancestors: The Journey Northwards

The year that Rose Chibambo was born, 1928, marked about one hundred years since her paternal ancestors, the Ngoni, had left their homeland, which is present-day South Africa. The actual year is not specified. Some scholars, such as late Malawian historian DD Phiri, will cite 1818 as the year in which the Zulu King, Shaka, defeated several tribes, including that of Zwangendaba, who was the leader of the group that came to be known as Ngoni.[i] Their departure would then have occurred after the defeat. TJ Thompson suggests that the defeat by Shaka was in 1819, and he notes a variation of dates for the Great Trek, or *Mfecane*, as any period between 1819 and 1825.[ii]

The Ngoni left because of conflict with Shaka Zulu. They also fled famine in search of more land and food to accommodate and feed a growing population. There is consensus, however, on the year that the Ngoni crossed the Zambezi River. Yet there are differences about whether the crossing occurred during October or November. References to 20 November may be more accurate, since the historical records refer to an eclipse which occurred at the time of the crossing, and there was a solar eclipse on 20 November 1835.[iii]

The group was composite from the start, including Swazi, Ndwandwe, Qabe and Ntungwa groupings. It would become even more mixed during the years spent wandering because of the Ngoni's interactions with other tribal groupings in the different places they stayed. There was, for instance, a period when Zwangendaba's group stayed in Mozambique, Tanzania and Zimbabwe. Some people were taken as captives on the journey, while others decided to join the Ngoni on their own accord. The group finally settled in Mzimba in the period between 1850 and 1855, defeating the Tumbuka who were living in the area. The Ngoni's influence on the Tumbuka is evident in some traditions, such as the custom of *lobola*, or bride-price, and the dominance of the patrilineal system. The influence was not one-dimensional; through intermarrying, future generations of the Ngoni would go on to speak ChiTumbuka more than ChiNgoni. This also reflected the fact that few people knew how to speak ChiNgoni because of the group's composite nature.

Chibambo's father was a Ngoni. Her mother, Nyaharaba, was a Tumbuka. However, Chibambo refers to herself as a Ngoni because of the patrilineal system in both Ngoni and Tumbuka societies.

One thing that the Ngoni were known for during their early years in Mzimba was raiding, driven by economic motivations, which, as Thompson suggests, included food and cattle. However, by 1897, changing values would help curtail the practice of raiding. The wage economy, brought in by the British administration, meant, as John McCracken has pointed out, that 'young men of warrior age were implicitly rejecting raiding as a primary occupation.'[iv] Missionaries were also influential and they first came into contact with the Ngoni in 1878. As a result of this influence, many Ngoni, including Chibambo's father, would go on to become Christians.

As has been the case with many other tribes during the colonial period, there are aspects of Ngoni culture that disappeared along the way, whereas others have persisted. For instance, Al Mtenje and Boston Soko have pointed out that since the Ngoni tended to focus on political dominance, this was often gained at the expense of several cultural aspects, such as language. The influence of the missionaries also led to the curtailing of traditional practices such as the *Incwala* dance. This particular dance was practised during the drought and involved slaughtering a black bull. If the bull urinated before being slaughtered, this was regarded as a sign that rain would fall in the village.[v] The *Incwala* dance has since been revived, although it is mostly performed in Zambia, with Malawian Ngoni chiefs travelling to attend the event. Government policy has also impacted Ngoni culture. For instance, Ngoni chiefs were detained for some hours in 2018 on their way to Zambia for the *Incwala* ceremony because they were wearing animal skins.[vi] Persistent aspects of Ngoni culture have included songs, dances, initiation rites, the naming of villages, people, cattle and dogs, as well as the integration of Ngoni vocabulary into ChiTumbuka.[vii]

LOMATHINDA

Chapter 2

Moving into Family Roles
1920s–1940s

LOMATHINDA

FAMILY ROLES

You know, I would also say that my father instilled the sense of education in the children of his brothers. And he made sure...he was paying school fees for them. He was actually the second-born in his family. He came from a family in which his father had married extra wives—and there were children in those families.

So even after he had gone for his education and he had come back, my father made sure that his brothers, even though they were married, must also go to school, so that they can learn how to read the Bible and write.

Quite an influential man.

He was. He was, really.

So, what I'm getting from this is that you said the children of his brothers...were these children also staying with your family at the time?

It was a village. It was such a big village...you have never seen...we were from the Ngoni clan. So in those days the Ngonis, the villages were so big. (*Softly, reflectively, counting:*) Agogo Lowole, Agogo Mhango, Kandulu, Kagulumbizi, the Lowoles were two... AgoNyoni...his father had six wives. So in all these families, there were children. My father took these children as his responsibility.

Now, with my mother, my mother was just a very good housewife, but she was also able to read and write. She could understand English. She had lived with an uncle who was a cousin of her father. That uncle of hers was one of the people who also had early education, and he used to work in the Mandala shops.[2] So she used to live with him, and he made sure that she went to school and she was able to read and write.

What do you remember about her? Was she a disciplinarian...?

Eh! She was. (*Laughs.*) My mother was a disciplinarian. That is very true. She was. Very strong. (*Laughs.*) In most cases, you know, as girls in the villages, we would... sometimes... In the areas, we used to have dams. Natural dams. Then it was a habit of girls that some certain times, we would like to go and swim, go and bath...then

---

[2] Mandala stores were shops opened across Malawi by the African Lakes Company (ALC), a Glasgow transportation and trading company, which was managed by brothers John and Fred Moir, who followed on the heels of Scottish missionaries. Owen JM Kalinga and Cynthia A Crosby write in the *Historical Dictionary of Malawi,* "[p]opularly known as Mandala because John Moir wore glasses (*mandala*), the ALC had general trading establishments in almost all districts in the colony" (2001, p. 3).

we would all be there, swimming and so on.

But in most cases, my mother would not allow me to go and join a group of my fellow girls to go and do that. She had her own ideas why she didn't want me to go there. But once she sees me, because by the time we come back from there, our eyes are red, and with the drips of water (*laughs*) we never used to have towels to wipe ourselves. It means you are coming out of the water...the water is dripping... (*Laughs.*)

And everyone can see that—

Although you try (*laughs*) so that by the time you get home everyone could see *kuti* ah, ah, this one has been to the river, to a dam. So by the time I got home then I would pretend I hadn't been anywhere. She would say, 'Ah, why are your eyes red?'

Then I wouldn't answer, because she had warned me before not to go to these natural dams. Then I would keep quiet. And sometimes she would whip me. Mmm. She was very...she never stood any nonsense. No. Very strong character, so I had to follow her instructions. I would say...I listened, I obeyed. (*Laughs.*)

If we were to compare, what was your father's role in terms of discipline? Did he leave that to your mother or could any parent discipline a child?

Uhm, in most cases, all parents could discipline a child. But with me, as I was growing up, definitely the discipline was left to my mother.

My father....oh, he loved me so much. He would even...if food was cooked, and as Ngonis, usually, for the men, the food used to be carried to what we used to call *kusangweni*.

Sangweni used to be where all the men used to sit and talk, outside the *kraal*. All the men, after working in the evening, the late afternoons, would gather at a *sangweni* outside. If a man doesn't go to *sangweni*, he is a very strange person. But they would all gather at a *sangweni* so that when women cooked, food used to go there. And that's why even a child who was an orphan would not be known, because they all used to eat at the open. And everybody would take part.

But at the same time, according to Ngoni customs, the elderly would be eating separately. After the elderly people had eaten then they would leave something for the young ones to take over and continue.

But because my father was a teacher, at times he would come at awkward times, so that he would not have time to go to *sangweni*, which means that he might have his food at home. But even when he was taking his food at home, he would still call the young ones...the children, the boys from his brothers' families. He would call them to come and join him. And he would ask me to come and join them. I would be the only girl, and oh, I was a favourite of my father, so that he never used to beat me. Only once did he beat me. (*Laughs.*)

Do you remember why?

(*Laughs.*) What happened was that he bought me a very beautiful material. In those early days, we never used to wear dresses, it was *salu*. So he bought me some very beautiful material. It was big. But...you know, in the village...not everybody was lucky to have something. Some of them would just have something small, which they would wear, a little bit here (*gestures to the lower part of the body*) in those early days. So, I used to feel that that is how it should be. Why should I have this big one?

Oh.

I should also wear what the others wear. So I went behind the house, made fire, and then, I put—because I didn't have a pair of scissors then I got some fire—

Oh no.

Burning, little by little, little by little. Then I tore it, on each side I tore it. So after tearing it up then I also wore the small pieces...just to be like everyone else.

So on that particular day, when my mother saw me, she said, 'What have you done?'

I couldn't answer...

So then evening came, we ate, my dad was not there. So I went, after my mother of course had scolded me. So much. She didn't beat me.

I used to sleep at my grandmother's house. So evening came then I went to my grandmother, and I slept.

We're talking about your paternal grandmother here?

Yes, the mother of my father. So, then my father came, after Mummy had reported to him. So he said, 'Where's she?'

'Ah, here she is, sleeping.' He said, 'Wake her up.' Then they woke me up. So he said, 'Where's that material? Where's that material that I bought you?' and I was quiet.

He said, 'I want to see it.' So I said, 'This is what I did.'

He said, 'Oh. You think everybody, those that wear this, that's how it should be? Don't you know that they are also in need but it's because they can't find it?'

Then he whipped me. (*Laughs.*) Literally whipping me.

Then my grandmother said, 'Ah, please forgive her. She knows she has made a mistake.' He said, 'No, she has to know that this is totally wrong.' That was the first time my father whipped me. (*Laughs.*)

Changing Times, Changing Space

In 1938, Margaret Read,[3] who had done extensive research on the Ngoni, published a journal article about the tribe's moral code. The article focused on the past traditions of the Ngoni, traditions lamented because they were no longer practiced, as well as those that had survived the test of time. Of note is when Read discusses the way in which girls dressed:

> In these early days of childhood excessive modesty was enjoined on small girls who were given a scrap of cloth or leather to hang down over their genitals or to wear as a small skirt. This cloth they were taught to smooth down when they sat so that their genitals were always covered.[i]

Read refers to a period after the Ngoni had settled in Mzimba, but before they had been incorporated into the British Central Africa (later Nyasaland) Protectorate of 1891. Yet several decades later, in the 1940s, Chibambo refers to a similar mode of dressing, which had become a way of life among Ngoni children. It would therefore appear that economic reasons notwithstanding, the strip of cloth had become part of traditional dress for children. The long material which Ziba had bought for his daughter was a sign of the changing times, one which the young Lomathinda still had to come to terms with.

Chibambo refers to the *sangweni* as part of the Ngoni culture that was still prevalent during her time. Again, the way in which her father attended the *sangweni*, sometimes choosing to forgo that particular space altogether, is a reflection of a culture that was at a crossroads. DD Phiri, for instance, describes the *sangweni* as an example of 'in-built social welfare services':

> Each family would send *ngwembe*, a wooden plate of food to the eating-place. Men ate first and then invited the *bafana*, boys, to come and eat the left-overs. Because of communal eating orphans never faced starvation. Women had a communal eating place of their own.[ii]

Similarly, Read emphasises the role played by the *sangweni* in the Ngoni social structure. She describes it as a place where 'the big men ate together and handed out what was left of their food to the boys.'[iii] Besides it being a communal food place, Read also emphasises the role of the *sangweni* as a place where men discussed stories of war and heroism.

Aaron Ziba, the primary school teacher, who was also a product of Livingstonia Mission, is an example of a generation that found itself having to make a compromise. Since, in Chibambo's words, a man who did not attend the *sangweni* was regarded as 'strange,' this was a part of his life that he did not cut out. But faced with a busy work schedule, there would be times when Ziba would not be with the men and would introduce some fluidity into the code of 'men only' by eating with his daughter.

---

[3] Read was assisted by Yesaya Mlonyeni Chibambo, Edwin's father and Rose's father-in-law.

Chapter 3

The Night Walk
1930s—1940s

THE NIGHT WALK

My relationship with my grandmother was quite good...the women used to eat together, we used to go to grandma, all of us. We would sit together with grandma, my mother and us, the children. We would eat together. In my time, that's how it was.

My grandmother was not very much a storyteller. But where you go wrong, she would only give you instructions. She would only give you instructions, 'That's not the way how we do things; we do things this way.'

One strange thing that happened: at that time, I think I was about...I must have been around eight years old or so. I was coming from my mother's house; it was now late in the evening. Going to sleep at my grandma's.

I was walking from my mother's house, going to my grandfather's house...because the village was so big, and my grandmother's house was in the middle.

So I would walk from my mother's house, which was sort of at the corner of their whole village, because in Ngoni, we used to build our homes in circles, really a circle; the first row, second row, third row, and according to the families. So that in the right end, the *kraal* would be there. Where the kraal is, the gates of the kraals would be facing the bush, so that when the cows come out, they just go. And then, the *kraal*...of course it wouldn't be far from the people's home...but wherever it ends...the *kraal*, there are no houses this side.

But on the end of the right-hand side, there are people who are *izinduna*. And on the left too, it's the *izinduna*. So that at the middle are the owners of the village.

And the role of the izinduna*?*

The role of the *izinduna* is to give advice to the village headman. Whenever anything happens, if there's anything that has happened, or someone wants to reach the village headman, he has to go through these people. He will have to explain to them what has happened; they are the ones who will explain to the village headman.

So, one day I was walking from my mother's house, going up to my grandma. As I was walking, right in the middle, from the east,...it was dark...I saw something like a big ball, very large, and it went with a sound, *du-du-du-du*, it went. The whole area was just light. The light went round and I ran. I just exclaimed, 'We-e-e!' I ran, went into my grandmother's house. But I saw it moving, going up, going up, until to the east, west. And it went with a big sound.

I went and...I just went in the house. I ran...fell down, just said, 'Ah.' After some time, then my grandmother said, 'What has happened?' I couldn't talk. She said 'Hey, *wena*, what has happened?'

Then I explained, I said, 'I've seen a big light, a big ball, but it gave a great light. I don't know whether it is the moon, it's falling, I don't know what it is'. I was so surprised.

So the following day, some people said...they were talking about it other villages too, they were talking about it. They said, 'Ah, yes, we saw the...something like a light.'

I don't know what it was...it was like something had dropped from somewhere. Up to this day I can't explain what it was. But this was one of the miracles that I saw during my time. They said, 'Ah, it is dark, now what is this here?' So I thought *kuti* ah, I don't know. But it frightened me.

The Flying Object

What did Lomathinda see that night on her way to her grandmother's hut? It is not easy to tell. There is, however, the following entry concerning Mtola in Mzimba, in Monica Grady's *Catalogue of Meteorites*:

> Mtola
>
> Mzimba district, Malawi.
>
> Fall 1944, June 17, 10 hrs.
>
> Stone.
>
> Approx. recovered weight: 1.08 kg.
>
> A single stone weighing about 2lb 603 (1.1 kg) was recovered. The specimen was in the Geological Survey Mus. but is now lost.[i]

The name Mtola was given to the stone because of the place it fell. MJ Crow states that Inkosi M'belwa II wrote to the Mzimba District Commissioner to report "the fall of a stone from heaven at Mtola Nyanjagha village"[ii] on 17 June 1944 at 17.00. According to Crow, the meteorite was never fully described and may have been among objects that were discarded when the Geological Survey moved to Liwonde in 1955.

Was that the stone Lomathinda saw as the meteorite fell and kept rolling? The year itself is not precise; it could be from the late thirties to the early forties. The time of the sighting poses a challenge to this theory. She saw the stone at night, but the catalogue indicates that the stone fell at 10 o'clock in the morning. The Mtola record is the only one of a meteor falling in the region, but there could be other explanations, still to be established, about what fell from the sky on that night.

Chapter 4

Remembering Recreation

1930s–1940s

W e used to dance what we used to call *Mchoma* or *Ndora*. During the moonlight. We would gather boys and girls; we would really be dancing. Clapping our hands and dancing.

Apart from that, *Ingoma*. Because with *Ingoma* we used to dance in the *kraal*. Yes, in the kraal. Then the boys would go in, sometimes with the elders too, especially when they are planning that they want to go and entertain a certain village or take part in a competition. So then they had to practice. Right in our village. So then we would go in with the young men. Usually, with *Ingoma*, the women would be clapping hands and singing. And then the men would be dancing.

So do you remember any particular songs?

Oh. (*Laughs.*)

At least one or two that you could recall.

Ah. (*Laughs.*) Oh dear. (*Clears throat.*) We used to sing, quite many of them.

Okay, but there must have been a favourite.

(*Laughs.*)

Okay, even if you don't sing it, at least if you could just tell me one particular song.

I can't tell you without singing it. (*Laughter.*) I can only tell by singing. I have so many, but the one that I remember most is 'Uingwe Jere.'

(*Sings:*)

Uingwe uingwe Jere.

Then the men would be saying, '*Ho, yawo eh. Uingwe ukhanyisa mawara njee.*'

We would all…there comes a time when men and women would correlate. Then the women would sing:

Uingwe Jere
Hoyawo
Uingwe ukhanyisa mawara njee. Uingwe mzira.

These are the men now. Saying, '*Uingwe mzira.*'

Uingwe Jere
Ho yawo.

Those that are saying *Ho yawo*, are the men now.

Uingwe ukhanyisa mawara njee.
Ayi mpulupulu uyingwe
Ho. Uyingwe ukhanyisa mawara njee.
Ayi chimutu nga uingwee.
He. Uyingwe ukhanyisa mawara njee.
Uyingwe mzira.

(*Laughs.*) *Uingwe* is a leopard. So it is the women actually calling for the men that there's *uingwe*, there's a leopard. So, insulting the men that there's a leopard out there. When they say, *chimutu nga uingwe*, saying *nkosi*, the chief's head is like that of a leopard. *Uingwe Jere, ukhanyisa mawara*. It's showing the...the...what would I say, *mawara*. You know, the leopard has got all those spots. It's partly a..ah..what would I say? Sort of... uplifting him.

The Inkosi?

The *Inkosi*.

So it has a significance beyond the leopard...

Yes, it has got a significance connecting to the *Inkosi*.

There was also what they used to call *vidokoni*. Of course, *vidokoni*, these are the things that even elderly would be saying...it is a story-telling. But telling it in a different way.

The women and the men would dance to *Mchoma* and even *Ndora*.

The Leopard in Ngoni Culture

The image of the leopard is multifaceted in Ngoni culture. Legend has it that the first M'mbelwa to be installed as chief in Mzimba was placed on the back of a captured leopard to symbolise his authority. TJ Thompson makes reference to this legend in his study of the interactions between the Northern Ngoni and Christian missionaries.[i]

The song 'Uingwe Jere' reflects the link between the leopard and royalty. It makes a contrast between the men of the village and the strong chief. By implication, the men are not as strong as the chief, which explains why Chibambo talks about the song insulting the men and uplifting the chief. It also underscores the society's expectation that a chief should be strong and, perhaps, distinctive, which accounts for the reference to the spots.

And yet, to quote Lupenga Mphande's translation of a different Ngoni praise song, the leopard can be 'something else.' In the context discussed by Mphande, the leopard becomes associated with danger, in the sense of dangerous alliances, especially for a people made vulnerable during the long journey to the north:

> Who has encountered a leopard on his left side
>
> He says the leopard will help me; whereas the leopard is something else.[ii]

Here, the leopard cannot be trusted. Another unfavourable attribute associated with a leopard is that of anger. This can be seen in one of the songs collected by Read, in which a woman is warned against being jealous. As per Read's translation:

> Behold, woman of jealousy,
>
> Thou art a leopard.[iii]

The word thus turns on itself, amassing both positive and negative connotations. In the end, it is a challenge to box a leopard into a particular category, and to even possess that leopard. The closest one comes to such possession is through metaphorical allusions or to the leopard skin on the floor or as part of traditional dress.

Chapter 5

Duties in the Kitchen and Maize Field 1930s and 1940s

DUTIES IN THE KITCHEN

At that time, during my time, we would eat *nsima* with beans or vegetables or with meat occasionally. Although they used to have so many cows—the Ngonis of my time—they would not kill them anyhow. A cow would be killed sometimes if there is hunger, and they want to exchange it with maize. Or sometimes they would kill a cow, quite often if there's a funeral of a grown up person.

So what was regarded as quality food?

Quality food was just *nsima* and beans. And vegetables. And during the rainy season, during the rainy season it was fresh vegetables, and then mushrooms, all kinds of vegetables.

During the rainy season used to be a good time, because there are so many vegetables that are planted, but also in the bush we used to know some of the leaves which were edible. And during the dry season, they used to preserve vegetables, they would dry them and put them into...preserving them in leaves of *masuku*. Then they would tie them up and hang them properly. Sometimes they used even to dry them up with tomatoes and so on. But mostly it used to be nutritious because they would not cook vegetables without groundnuts. They would always cook vegetables, either dry or fresh, still groundnuts must be added. They would pound the groundnuts and then add them to the vegetables.

So at least every girl had to know how to cook and how to preserve vegetables.

Yes. Exactly. Because one had to learn it from the parents. Whenever her mother is doing that, every girl must take part.

The role of the girl was to do the pounding and the cooking, because we didn't have *zigayo* in those days. And then the role of a boy was to make sure that he goes to look after cattle.

My brother who came after me, he was looking after cattle. And then going into the garden, that was also the duty of a boy. But girls, too, would go to the garden. That is after they had done their pounding, and they would cook and follow the people who go to the garden, which is the role that I played so much.

So you grew up knowing the roles you were supposed to play?

Oh yes...when my father goes to the garden with my mum—they would go together—they would give instructions to say, 'You will have to cook, take care of the child. You will have to cook and follow us to the garden with food.'

Each time after I had done everything, then I would go to the garden to give them food because you had to pack all the food in a basket. Water, foodstuff. Of course this would be after you have also gone to draw water to come and do the cooking. If there was no flour, you have to do the pounding as well with (*chuckles*) your sister on your back. And then after that you have to do all the cooking. Then pack up the food... Our gardens never used to be near the village. You had to walk up a certain distance.

Once I bring them that food...then my father would say, 'Now we are going to sit down to eat. But you start...you take over.' They would give me some space and say, 'From here, you reach up there, you do...you also cultivate the land. This is your space.' Then I would take the child, give it to my mother. They would now start eating, and I take over the hoe, cultivating.

You are talking about you, but then those boys who had been born before, the children who had been born before from your father's family. They must have been there as well...

There was one boy. At this time, they had grown, and, as grown-ups, he would be hoeing, but after he had grown up, he got married and went away to look for employment.

The three girls from the previous family?

They were married.

Okay. So...this was the young girl, taking food to the garden, but then afterwards having to cultivate while others are eating...how did you feel about that?

I accepted it as part of my duty.

The Cow and its Role in Ngoni History

The previous chapter made reference to the leopard in all its ambiguity. When it comes to the cow in Ngoni culture, there are no such ambiguities; a family's prestige was determined by the number of cows that family had.

The *Mfecane* was driven by groups seeking to acquire more grazing land; another aspect was that warriors would take cows from the targeted villages during the raids. Cows were part of the homestead; men ate behind the *kraal*, dances could be held in the same *kraal*, the bride price was paid for in cattle. To be without cows was, literally, to be vulnerable; even the shield used during battles was made from leather. Chibambo's recollection illustrates that it was more important to keep the cows than to have beef as a daily part of one's diet; given its importance, the cow was saved for special occasions.

With the onset of colonialism, cows continued to be of significance to the Ngoni. It was from the sale of cows that households could pay tax and school fees. Cows were especially important because there was no major cash crop, such as cotton, tobacco or tea, in the Northern Region, unlike the Central and Southern Regions. McCracken reports that there was potential for cotton growing in Karonga, but when the cotton was attacked by the pink bollworm in 1925, government banned cultivation in the Northern Region up until the 1930s.[i]

Rearing cattle may have been a source of livelihood, but it came with its share of challenges. The rinderpest outbreak of 1892 and the tick-borne East Coast fever of 1926 stand out among challenging times. The fever actually led to the banning of cattle exports from Northern Malawi until 1930.[ii] The 1920s were also a time when cattle in the Northern Region were plagued by the tsetse fly.[iii]

There has, understandably, been a lot of focus on cattle and its economic and cultural value among the Ngoni. However, the Ngoni of Northern Malawi also practised subsistence farming. As Chibambo has stated above, vegetables were also a very important part of the Ngoni diet. In his analysis of Ngoni agricultural methods, TJ Thompson observes that while writers such as Donald Fraser might cast doubt on Ngoni agricultural activity,[iv] there is evidence that the Ngoni not only made and sold agricultural equipment, but also were well organised as far as crop production was concerned.[v] As Thompson points out, the Ngoni, often criticised for supposedly having poor agricultural skills, were still the same group that had produced 22 varieties of vegetables in one village alone.

Chapter 6

Travelling with Childhood Companions
1930s–1940s

CHILDHOOD COMPANIONS

Y ou know, I was a very funny person perhaps. I was a little shy. But at the same time, as I was growing up, I hated to disappoint someone. And I hated to be disappointed, too.

Ah, as I was growing up, from the village, we were so many girls. But I was one of the young girls. Well, at the village, I was second to the big girls, and then there was my niece, who was the youngest. So my niece was my close friend, because we were sort of almost the same age as the big girls. The big girls, they were bullying us. (*Laughs.*)

So your niece, what was her name?

She was Ethel. She's late.

So you were very close to Ethel?

Yes. But we parted; she didn't go far with school. We parted when I went to boarding school. Though she was younger to me, she got married first.

You talked about the big girls who were bullying you. What forms of bullying went on?

(*Laughs.*) No, it wasn't quite much of bullying. But, you know, they would not like you to join their talk because we were young. Then they would say, 'Ah, how do you know this? Why are you joining?'

They always wanted us to keep quiet and listen to them. (*Laughs.*)

So apart from your parents and your grandmother, who else would you say had an influence on you when you were growing up? Who else acted as a parent?

Uhm, it was very strange. My sister, Grace, the second born of my father, had gotten married. She didn't have children. But she came to pick me up. From the time I was six, she would take me. Of course she would come and ask Mum and say, 'I want this child with me.'

So I would go and stay with her for quite a time. She was married to a son of a sub-chief...Jere. Khwechisa we called him. And I stayed with her for quite some time. I would go back home but she would still come to pick me up and so on.

So, later, her husband left for South Africa in search of jobs, which used to be the case with many Malawians. And he was there for a long time. So then she decided to leave, because years had passed, and he had written her that he might not come back. So she took that letter to his father and said, 'This is the letter that he has written, therefore I'm going back to my village.'

Her mother-in-law cried so much. And so then, when she was ready to leave the village, my sister said, 'Ah, let's go and say goodbye to Father-in-law. We should go back home.' So we went and I sat near her. So she said to them, 'Well, I have packed up my *katundu* at home. I'm leaving.'

So we left and went back to our village. But later on she got married again. She still (*laughs*) she still came to pick me up. That time, I was then eight years old. She was now married to an Elliard Chindi.

So while we were there, I became very ill. I was sleeping at a certain family's house and one time when I slept, I felt as if somebody was sitting on me. And I tried to get up, I couldn't. I tried hard to get up, I couldn't. Then, when morning came, I felt that I was sick. So when I went back to the house my sister said, 'Ah, but what's wrong with you today? You don't seem to be happy.' So I said, 'I'm not feeling well. I'm sick.'

I explained to her how I felt during the night. I slept the whole day until evening, I thought that was now morning. I said, 'Is it morning?' She said, 'No, it's only now that it's getting dark.'

I said, 'No, I don't want to sleep again.'

But I went on for the full week. I wasn't getting any better. So then the man she was married to said, 'We'd better take this child back home.' So they took me back to my parents... They tried all types of medicine, our roots. The hospital was too far, there was no transport, so they were just looking for our natural medicine. I tell you, I didn't get better. The whole year, I was sick. And any medicine they were giving me, I was vomiting. Until, they just decided...they had to leave me in the village, and they would go to the garden, work, and then they would come back later.

So, until one of my cousins, who had gone to Harare in search of a job, came back. He had been gone for a long time, but he came back. So when he came back, that time, I was just...I don't know what it was, really. I was just getting sickly, sickly. Although I was walking, I was not myself. I would feel better in the morning, but when it comes to lunchtime, I'm not well. I would go to school in the morning, in the afternoon I'm back, I'm sick. It went on for some time. And I became so thin.

So one of the days my cousin was just monitoring me, monitoring me. Then he called me, and said, 'Can you come home?' So I went to his house. I don't know whether he had discussed it with father or mother, I don't. But he just called me; he said, 'Come home.'

So I went to his house, and then he took his medicine. That medicine was in...ah...a tin of shoe polish. Then he cut me here and here (*gestures to the face, the back, the arms, the feet*). So then after he had done the cutting, then he rubbed in that medicine. Then said, 'It's alright, you go home.'

Then I went. From that time, I was better. I was cured. I tell you, I was cured with that medicine. I don't know what it was. I said, 'Ah.' It was black, and as if he had put in some oil. It was a miracle.

Was he a medicine man or herbalist?

No, he wasn't known to be a herbalist. He had just returned from Harare, from wherever he went to work. And he had been home of course, by this time, he had been there for some months since his return. But I don't know whether he got this medicine from somebody too, wherever he was, but it cured me. And it was that medicine that cured me. Otherwise I was dying. Honestly! From that time I was alright.

Do you remember your father's reaction when he was told what had happened?

No, they didn't even ask me. He must have discussed it with them.

But he was such a wonderful cousin. Very responsible man.

What was his name?

He was Ophaniel Ziba, born of the brother of my father. The eldest brother of my father. He was another very responsible man. Because even when my father was doing cooperative,[4] Ophaniel was the one who was helping him.

Even when my brother, who came after me, suffered an illness, it was him who tried very much to assist. But I think by that time, ah, I don't think he had that medicine, because it was now after some years, and I was at boarding.

I have noticed your earlobes have holes, not like the tiny piercings for those who wear earrings. These holes are quite big. Is there a story behind them?

These earlobes were a sign of identity that you are a Ngoni. After piercing, you had to put in something. They used to put in a reed. The man who used to do it would cut some small reeds to put into the earlobe, because blood would be coming out. So you put the reeds in so that the lobe doesn't close. The reeds would stay in until the lobe heals. Then the hole remains. So when the hole gets smaller, you change reeds, put in a bigger reed. You keep on changing, to make the hole bigger. Because the idea was that it must be big. At the end of it, you put in a....*nyanga ya njobvu*...an ivory bracelet.

They used to shape it in such a way that it would fit here (*gestures to the ear*) and make

---

[4] In Chapter One, Chibambo explains that after retiring from teaching, her father opened a dairy. She also points out that it was a government requirement for dairy farmers to work as a team or a cooperative. It is to that partnership amongst the farmers that she refers here.

you beautiful.

So boys and girls would do this?

Boys didn't put in reeds; it was only girls. Boys would use what was known as *vikono*, more like a bracelet.

But the cutting, wasn't it painful?

Oh it was. Very painful.

What did he use?

He used *ka* knife…a very sharp knife, *mxamati*.

So that was the reason my father didn't want me to do it. He said, 'No, you should not cut it.'

So how did you do it?

I had to sneak out of the house. I did it secretly. My friends were laughing at me. My age-mates had all done it, and they were laughing at me. They used to say *gulumuntira*. It is a way of saying you are blind.

Wachigulumuntira. So without kuboola, they would mock you.

But that was beauty in those days. Very important. So because my friends kept on laughing at me, I said, 'Ah, why should I remain alone?' Then I sneaked out, early in the morning with others. Because the man was not at our village; it was quite at a distance, and you had to be there early in the morning when it's still cold. My father didn't know. I went with my friends, then they cut me. I came back. And now blood was oozing.

Mummy saw it, 'Where did you go? Who did it? How did you go alone? But you know what Dad said about this. Oh, you will see.'

And when my dad saw it, 'Who did this?'

And he knew the man. He said, 'I'm going to scold him. I told you not to do this. Now why did you do it?'

I said, 'My friends were laughing at me.'

So then he kept quiet. He didn't go to the man to scold him. My father understood that it was really just me...that man was innocent.

So that's how I had these piercings. My father said, 'Don't put in anything,' he wanted them to close up. I said no. I didn't want them to close up. Ya. So it used to be real beauty. You could only do it, say, from ten up to around about twelve. If you were older than that, they would refuse.

Earlobe Piercings among the Ngoni

The following stories show some of the perspectives on earlobe piercing among the Ngoni:

Everybody used to have those piercings: my parents, my grandparents. You know how we missed it? In 1949, I was only five, so they said no. They sent us back, they said, 'You're too young.' They used to have a very sharp knife; *mxamati*. But I had *vikono*; those were like iron bracelets, although you could bend them, unlike iron. People would wear *vikono* on their arms, and sometimes around their necks. It was beautiful. Some weeks ago, we were laughing at how some men would actually use *fuko*, a snuff box. They would fit it into the earlobe and be moving around, especially if the man had no place in which to keep the snuff.[i]

In contrast with the neighbouring peoples, the Ngoni had no facial or body markings, and it was the pierced ears which showed that they were true Ngoni. In the days of warfare, captives, especially boys and men, were forcibly made to have their ears pierced.[...]

Children of Ngoni families, as also these others, chose their own time to have their ears pierced, though sometimes their father or father's sister or father's mother reminded them that it was about time. It was nearly always soon after the second teeth had come, and children who delayed having it done were taunted by their fellows: 'You, are you afraid, my age-mate? See my ears already have bone in them.' This was a reference to the round plugs of bone inserted when the hole was large enough. A bit of thread was put in at first, then a small bit of grass, then a fine reed, and finally a bone plug. Ear piercing was always done in the cold weather so that the lobe of the ear would heal quickly. It was carried out by a leading woman of one of the Ngoni families, who watched the children to see how they took it. They knew it was a test of courage, and however much they were afraid it would hurt, they stood like little statues during the operation, with a face as set and expressionless as when they were being beaten.[ii]

There is also the story of Chanda Mukulu, wife of a Ngoni chief, Mperembe Jere, during the mid-nineteenth century. She is said to have had piercings so large that a hand could pass through them.[iii]

CHILDHOOD COMPANIONS

Chapter 7

In Search of Education
1930s—1940s

IN SEARCH OF EDUCATION

You know, in those early days of our school, our schools used to be called village school. So in our village schools, we used to start with what we used to call *borodi*. *Borodi* meant that we used to write on the floor, outside, on the sand. We had no books...

And then I started my school at Kafukule Village School. I went up to Class 4 in those days. We used to say 'Class.' Class 4, where we used to read *Kasepuka na ka Sungwana*. That was a very important book. Then when I was doing *Kasepuka na ka Sungwana*, all the girls at the village—most of those big girls at the village—had dropped out of school. They said, 'Ah, we are grown up, we cannot keep on going to school.'

I was more or less left alone going to school. But I was not deterred. I decided that I would still be going to school. Of course, my mum and my dad, too, they helped me, because they insisted, 'You have to go to school.'

Whereas for my friends, it meant nothing to their parents, even if they stopped school. So I was alone, going to school, until I finished my vernacular class.

Which lasted until Four or...?

Until Four.

So it would be you and a number of boys in the village.

It would be me with some of the boys. And then after I had done that, luckily enough I passed. But when I passed, I don't know how I was influenced that I should go to Ekwendeni, to go and start Standard One.

Oh, so 'Class' and 'Standard'—

They were different. Standard, it's where we were going now to start English. From Class One to Class Four, it was only Tumbuka. And the books we used to read were Tumbuka.

Okay. So off you went to Ekwendeni.

Yes. Then I went to Ekwendeni Girls' School. No, I should say, to a girls' boarding. But the school itself was actually a co-education school.

What age would you have been at the time you were going to Ekwendeni?

At the time I went to Ekwendeni, I was thirteen years old. Rather I should say I was thirteen and a half, because on my birthday, to reach fourteen, I was already at

Ekwendeni, doing my Standard One.

It was a new place, and, as boarders, first, we had a boarding mistress, an assistant boarding mistress. Perhaps she had some influence on me, because she was a cousin of my mother, and she happened to be an assistant boarding mistress. And she came from Kafukule itself. Our senior boarding mistress was Miss Walker, Betty Walker.

She was very good, but very protective, I must say. Then we started our education. As we were, in the morning, when we went to school, h-e-e. (*Laughs.*) We would wake up very early in the morning, get ready and then march. We would be marching on the line, going to chapel. Then after prayers in the chapel, we go straight to school.

That's how it used to be. Every day. And if you're late, you're in trouble.

What kind of trouble?

Well, you will be punished. You were sent to draw water to fill up some tins. And we used to walk almost about two miles to a river to draw water. We used to do our own cooking.

We used to have two streams at school and that helped us. We would take turns; there were those that used to go in the morning, and then those that used to go in the afternoon are the ones who would be doing the cooking. They would do the cooking and by the time those come that had gone in the morning, then we all eat. The afternoon ones would have to rush to go to school. Those that had come back from school would have to make sure that there was water, and we would go and draw water from the river, Nyangwa.

But it used to be a very long way. And to carry four gallons of water, it used to be hell. But it helped us to grow strong. Those that were lazy from their houses back home, who never used to work, found it very hard. But for some of us, it wasn't that hard.

And on Saturdays, we had to go and bring firewood. And also we would be doing pounding by ourselves, and others would be going to *chigayo*. We used to have *chigayo*, which was manual. There was no electricity. But you have to keep on…

So times had indeed changed, because when we were talking about childhood, you told me that there was no form of chigayo.

Oh no, no.

But now things were changing somewhat…

This was a *chigayo* at a mission. Under the mission. There was no *chigayo* anywhere in any village in the rural areas. And this was a *chigayo*, manual. And it was something quite new to most of us, because it was almost...it was just breaking the maize. Not really smooth. No.

As long as it was broken, it was *mgaiwa*, that was enough. It wasn't the *mgaiwa* that we know today. Actually with big particles. (*Laughs.*) So that whoever was cooking, they would make sure that they use enough fire, cook it and let it simmer for a while so as to soften up all those big particles.

Did you have to take the food from home, or did the mission provide this food?

The mission used to provide some maize. But whenever we are coming from home, we would also bring something. It was not a must, but I think for some of us your conscience will tell you that you can't just go, you have to carry something, which used to be taken as part of the food at a boarding.

But definitely, the mission used to provide maize and beans for relish. It was only once sometimes, on a Sunday, that we would eat meat. Sometimes perhaps twice a month, but most of the relish we used to have was beans through and through.

Although I haven't surveyed much since I came back from exile, the boarding structure is still there. Although I don't think they are using it now. And the big house which used to house the mistress, it is still there. But things have gone down, somehow, which is very disappointing. Because as it used to be, we used to have this side, it's where you would have a dining hall and then a kitchen. And a store-room. So that the compound... the compound would be dividing the dormitory and the rooms where we used to sleep. Now in-between, it is a compound. So it is within this compound where most of the activities used to take place.

We used to have *mathuli na misi*. We used to pound our own maize if we wanted to eat maize flour. And maize flour, we ate it mostly on Saturdays and Sundays. The rest of the days we used to eat *mgaiwa*. And it is on Sunday that we would eat meat. But then on Saturday, early in the morning, we must go and look for firewood.

We would bring enough firewood to last the whole week. At the same time, we have to pound. We would pound maize, soak it. On a Wednesday, sometimes, we would do the pounding, just a little bit. But on Saturday, we would do the main pounding, so as to have flour ready for Saturday and Sunday.

How did you feel about this? I mean yes, you had worked at home, you had been hard-working, but this work was different from what you were doing at school.

Yes, it was different, but we accepted it. We had no choice. We accepted it.

Of course we had some friends who were lazy, but there was nothing they could do. If some of them had favours with the mistress, well, they would dodge...but some of us...I suppose it depends on how one was brought up, because some of us would feel it is a duty we had to do. And firewood, we used to go far down to go and look for firewood. And you have to carry big bundles, bringing them back to the boarding. After that, you have to go to the river, in order to get ready for the coming week. You have to wash your clothes and we used to wear boarding uniforms, which used to be khaki dresses, with a blue ribbon around the neck and the sleeves.

Did you have to buy this or was it provided by the mission?

It was provided by the mission. And we also used to participate as Girl Guides, and we used to have beautiful uniforms, provided by the missions.

On Sundays, we used to wear white clothes...a blouse top and *nsalu*, in the way it used to be worn in Malawi in those days. That's how we used to wear it. We would all wear white. Even the head would put on white.

Girl Guide uniform, what colour was it?

It was blue.

And what was the name of the boarding mistress?

Eritas Kumwenda. She went to school at Livingstonia. Her mother was working there as a cook, then she trained there. Eritas was a well-disciplined lady.

As I said, our school was beautiful...we had orange trees in the yard. And then we had to clean the whole yard inside and outside. And if anyone dodges, they used to be given punishment; you have to go and do the sisals. You know the actual sisal...and you have to go to the river, to make it into cotton. In order to do this, you go to the river, because there are rocks, so you beat it on the rocks, *pha-pha-pha*, until it is all gone. It's just clean cotton. But after that you have sores all over your body. From sisal.

Did you ever have to do that yourself? Did you ever have to go and beat sisal?

Yes, you actually had to go and do it, in order to bring out that sisal into cotton. It used to be part of a punishment if you do anything wrong.

So you were punished yourself?

I was never one of the people to be punished. (*Laughs.*) I was very obedient.

IN SEARCH OF EDUCATION

Did people like the boarding mistress eat different food from the food you were eating?

Ya, mmm....they used to eat their own food, they never used to eat *mgaiwa*. Very rarely, they used to ask us to prepare it for them, but they used to prepare it themselves. Anyway, with the white mistress, she had her own cooks. Our mistress, she used to cook her own food, and sometimes she would ask some of the girls to come and cook it for her.

Did the fact that you had to eat mgaiwa and beans affect your eating habits now?

It affected me in such a way that I never liked *mgaiwa*, nor do I like beans anymore. (*Laughs.*) Even now, I eat beans, but very rarely.

And school fees. What was the system like at the time?

We used to pay school fees. I remember at one time when I was doing my Standard Four, my father said that he didn't have the money. So when I came to school, I said, 'My father has said that he doesn't have the money anymore, so I don't know what I could do.' So the mistress—the white mistress—told me, 'You can bring anything that you have at home. You can bring either *mipini*, *vyakulimira*, or anything that will be converted into forms of money.' But eventually when I went back, my father gave me money.

I went to school during a period when girls had to keep their hair short at school and were not allowed to braid it. What was the situation during the time you were at school?

During our time it was the same thing. We used to cut our hair. All the time we would cut it, and we never used to wear shoes.

So you had these beautiful uniforms but—

No shoes. Even those who had shoes were not encouraged to wear them. I think, at that time, one reason was that not many were able to afford so it would be discouraging to some of the girls. Not only girls, because even at the boys' boarding, they all used to go to school without shoes. The idea was those who could not afford it, they may, you know, feel left out.

And the languages that were spoken at these boarding schools?

We used to speak our vernacular languages...except when we are speaking to the boarding mistress.

What particular subjects did you like?

Well, at school, my favourite subjects were...I used to love sums, because we had not yet started Mathematics at that time. Very little, but we were doing Arithmetic, and I loved English. I liked History and a little bit of Geography. These were mostly my favourite. We used to do Agriculture too, but very seldom. And we used to have...what was it called at that time...something to do with health...but it used to be very seldom, when someone from hospital would come to teach us.

I must say, when I look back, I was quite good in my subjects, because I used to be first or second. Since this was a co-ed, the boys used to mock me, because I would compete with them, so that, sometimes if it is not me being the first, it's a boy. And if the boy fails, it is me in class. So once it's me, if I'm one of the first, then the boys would be mocking. (*Laughs.*)

What would they say?

Ah, sometimes, when the teacher was asking questions, and everybody was quiet, I would answer the questions. Oh, once he went out, they would say, 'Even you girls, so you think you are something? So you think you are brighter than us all?' You know, that sort of thing. (*Laughs.*) Making you feel small. But I would say, 'So what? I have done it. You have failed.' (*Laughs.*) No, I wasn't bad.

Our teacher was Edward Kadonanga Gondwe, the father of Goodall Gondwe.[5]

The boys in my classroom felt insecure because our teacher, the old man, Mr Gondwe, would tease them too, and say, 'You can see the girl is able to do more things than you.' So then that used to make them feel a bit bad.

He was a very good teacher and a disciplined man. He believed in discipline.

So this marching that you talked about, was it only for the girls? Did the boys also march on their own?

Yes. The boys had their own boarding master. They had their own boarding, away from us. School, classes, we were together. But after that, those go to their own, the girls too go to their own.

In terms of age, the girls that were at your school, how did you relate to them?

In the school, we had some of the girls from the villages, and some of us who came from far were the ones who were at the boarding. We were boarders. No, the relationship was good.

---

[5] Goodall Gondwe is a Malawian politician. He trained as an economist and was Director of the Africa Division of the International Monetary Fund. He served as Minister of Finance from 2004 to 2009 in the late President Bingu wa Mutharika's cabinet and also from 2014 to 2019 in President Arthur Peter Mutharika's cabinet.

Um, of course you know sometimes, jealousy, they wouldn't show it much but you could see it, especially when it comes to dressing. Not all of us came from well-to-do families. So sometimes the grown-up girls would come when you're at school, and perhaps they are the ones who went in the morning first. They are back, and you are at school, now after that, in the afternoon, perhaps there is a chance for them to go to the shop, you find they have taken your clothes, they have put them on. In the hope that when they come back they will put it back before you come. Ah, I used to dislike that.

I see, but there was no teasing[6] like what we hear about these days, where those who come earlier tease the newcomers?

No, during my time we didn't have much teasing. But of course we had quite big girls, some of them who had been there perhaps three years before we came. But they used to respect themselves. But it is some of them—a few—who would still tamper with your clothes. (*Laughs.*)

During those days when you were at school, did you ever have such thoughts as, 'Why is the British government ruling us?' Did you wonder why the white people were there?

No. That time, I didn't wonder. It was just something I accepted. In fact, with us, because we had these missionaries, we never felt affected by sort of a feeling of colour bar. We just accepted them as they were and *nawo*, they are human beings in their own way, we are what we are, and especially in the mission, we were at a boarding. We just accepted our mistress that she's here...the mistress, to look after us. So I never had a feeling of saying, 'But why?' Ah ah.

Did you find it as something of an advantage that the boarding mistress was someone you knew?

Not at any time. I never even used to go to her house. Ah...when I look back, I think...I think I was too independent. I never liked to bother anybody. And I had no reason to bother anybody.

How long was the period you spent at the school?

I was at Ekwendeni for five years. I was there for five years and I liked it very much. Even during our holidays at home, I used to look forward to boarding school. The only thing I used to hate was beans. But otherwise, on the whole, I liked going to school.

When you went home for the holidays, how did it feel knowing that you were coming back to an area where some of the girls had dropped out?

---

[6] Teasing, in this context, refers to a form of hazing or making fun of newcomers in schools. In its extreme forms, it includes bullying.

I was very much alone at home. At that time, some of the girls had married. And others were a bit...looking at me as strange. (*Laughs.*) Because I remember one time when I was still going to my village school, when these big girls dropped out, it was in such a way that they said, 'Ah, we cannot go back to school. We are grown up now. There is no need of going back to school,' and talking in a very discouraging manner. I said, 'Ah, but me, I will still go to school.'

So when I was at a boarding, ah...they looked at it as being a very strange thing.

And then there were your siblings. Did they ever follow in your footsteps in terms of school?

Ya. Especially, there's one who...also followed. She did up to Standard Six, and then she got married. She didn't do a career, she got married. We were unfortunate, I think; we used to be proposed to fast. (*Laughs.*)

So you were unfortunate?

Ya. (*Laughs.*) Because once you are proposed to, then they plant in you wrong feelings altogether. Wrong thoughts, that after this it means I'm going to marry. You know, so you don't very much look forward to something else. (*Laughs.*) But our last born but one, at least she did...she improved herself. She did up to Form Five, and then she took a secretarial course. Of course her first career that she had chosen was to be a nurse. She was at Queen's, as a nurse. I should say I actually brought her up. But then because of the Cabinet Crisis[7] that had happened, when she was already at Queen's doing her nursing, when we left, things were not good for her. Because most members of the Youth League, they knew her. So they would go there, looking for her, Young Pioneers. And then the staff used to hide her that she's not here, kept on...so later on, I understand at the hospital they said, 'It will be very difficult for us to keep on hiding you. I think you better find your way out.'

So that's how she left. Then she followed me. She's Nellie. For a while she was there with me in Zambia. She did her secretarial course. After that, then she was working with the bank, as a secretary of the bank manager; after some years, she changed to banking.

---

[7] The Cabinet Crisis, which will be explained in detail in Chapter Fourteen, occurred in 1964. In summary, it was the escalation of tensions that had been building up between Dr Hastings Kamuzu Banda and his Cabinet Ministers since he became Prime Minister in 1963. Among the issues that triggered the Crisis were the Ministers' reactions to the delay in Africanisation of government institutions, Kamuzu's acceptance of the Skinner Report, which would reduce civil servants' salaries, the proposal for a fee in public hospitals, Kamuzu's refusal to forge relations with People's Republic of China (Peking)—preferring instead the pro-West Republic of China (Formosa)—and his cordial relationship with Portugal and apartheid South Africa. The Ministers presented their complaints to him in August 1964, and a month later, those who were regarded as ring-leaders were dismissed from Cabinet. The dismissed Ministers were Orton Chirwa, Augustine Bwanausi and Kanyama Chiume. Rose Chibambo, who was Parliamentary Secretary, was also dismissed. Ministers Yatuta Chisiza, Willie Chokani and Masauko Chipembere resigned from Cabinet in solidarity. The former Ministers were regarded as rebels and went into exile.

So she's still in Zambia?

She's still in Zambia, she got married. She married a Malawian, a man from Zomba. But when things were about to change in Malawi, the man wanted to come back to Malawi. When he came back home...he came alone, my sister...we were still at home, we were still trying to...test the waters, but then when he came back home, he didn't last long, he died. He died at his home in Zomba. *Kwa che Mwambo uko* (In Mwambo's village). (*Sighs.*) We came, we found him buried already. She had three boys with him. So she's still in Zambia, but she retired from work.

If you went to Ekwendeni at the age of about thirteen and a half, and if you stayed there for five years, that would mean you were there until you were around 18 or 17?

18.

So what happened? Why did you stay for five years?

I was going to school. I went up to Standard Five at that time. Then my fiancé-to-be, he was a teacher at Livingstonia. Because usually, in the way it was at school, when the girls reached Standard Four, most of them used to be sent to Livingstonia. So that they would be at Livingstonia but also training for their careers, planning for their careers, what type of career they want...and our main institution for the careers was Livingstonia. Because at Livingstonia you had all the departments; you had carpentry, you had building, you had secretarial, you had training as a teacher, you had nursing, they were all there at Livingstonia. So that if one had to choose, you would choose to be whatever you want to be at Livingstonia.

So the girls, even those in Standard Five, they would be at Livingstonia. But I was not allowed to go. I don't know, I think my mistress, especially the white one, whether she liked me, I don't know. But she was too protective; she didn't want me to go to Livingstonia because by then she had already known that I had a fiancé who was a teacher at Livingstonia. (*Laughs.*)

So after Standard Five, that was it. Then I got married. I got married, I never did anything. It was just from school to marriage.

So the mistress had a say; she was the one who could approve of your going somewhere for training?

Yes. She didn't want me to go to Livingstonia; she wanted me to keep on schooling at Ekwendeni, up to Standard Five. So if I passed Standard Five, only then could I have gone to Livingstonia. Because Standard Six was only in Livingstonia.

So it was possible for some girls to actually do Standard Four and then go to Livingstonia?

Yes.

So you did Standard Five, you passed Standard Five, and you did not go to Livingstonia.

No. I was in Standard Five. And it was more fitting at that time that I could have gone to Livingstonia, because now it was only the boys in Standard Five, and I was the only girl among 24 boys. It was a bit awkward, but I was there. Just because my fiancé, whenever he came, after the schools, or perhaps he's on holiday, he would still come to boarding. And he would never see me without begging from the mistress. Oh no. I would never see him unless he goes to beg from the mistress. No girls were allowed to get out anywhere.

Girls' Education in Nyasaland

It was not easy for African girls to attend classes during the colonial period in Nyasaland. While there was no law against going to school, there were many forces that girls came up against.

A girl from Nyasaland had to grapple with Victorian ideas from some of the missionaries. They felt that school should serve to prepare a girl for her role as a Christian wife.[i] Such missionaries therefore focused on subjects that they felt suited a girl's role, such as cooking, embroidery and needlework. Isaac Lamba notes:

> The proper education for the African woman, if any, was that which promoted her subservience to and dependence on the man, a situation often seen by westerners as conveniently fitting in the African milieu.[ii]

Even when girls had the chance to take the same subjects as boys, the question of co-ed or separate education came up. Some missionaries thought that if boys and girls were together in the same classroom, indiscipline among students would ensue.

Parents were also anxious about whether their daughters would get married, especially since education had disrupted what had been a predictable pattern before then: childhood, girlhood, courtship, marriage, motherhood. With the advent of education, the pattern was not as straightforward from girlhood to courtship. This is why female students such as Chibambo, who did not drop out, were regarded as strange during an era when many girls left school in order to get married.

Chapter 8

From the Classroom to Courtship

1940s

So *now that we have had several references to this fiancé, could you please tell me how you met?*

(*Laughs.*) It was very strange, you know. I had just come from the village, and I had started schooling. So my fiancé happened to be a son of a reverend, who was at that time a minister of the church. And it was actually at Ekwendeni itself.

And at that time the mission was, I tell you, mmm....things have gone down. And I sometimes wonder why. That mission used to be Mission. It used to be beautiful, with flowers and so on. And this was my father-in-law's work; he was really doing wonderful work to see to it that the surroundings are beautiful. Of course we had the missionaries themselves, but the mission station itself, he was controlling it.

So while he was there, then, my fiancé, Edwin, had finished doing his Standard Six at Livingstonia. He even did his teacher's training for two years; he had finished it. And then a secondary school had opened in Blantyre.

Blantyre Secondary School?

Yes. It was the first secondary school. He finished school when he was young, so when he heard that there was a secondary school in Blantyre, he said, 'Ah, I'm not teaching. I must go to secondary school.'

So when he came back from Livingstonia, he was at the mission, preparing to go to secondary school.

Our teacher was his brother, whom he came after.

So your teacher at Ekwendeni—

My class teacher at Ekwendeni was his brother. So I don't know whether it was by arrangement or not, because his brother had not yet married, but we knew that he had a fiancée, who was also a student. (*Laughs.*)

So then, one of the days, Edwin came to take over the class of his brother in the afternoon. Then he came in...so we said (*lowers voice*), 'Ah, maybe we have a new teacher today.' (*Laughs.*)

He came and then he gave us dictation. So we all wrote the dictation. It was the last subject. He gave us English dictation, this new teacher. (*Laughs.*) We were all giggling, 'Oh, he looks like our teacher, this man.' So those that knew them said, 'Yes, this is his young brother.'

So after we had done dictation, then he collected our notebooks and corrected them. He gave them back to us; I also got mine. Then, afterwards, he called back for my notebook. So I said, 'Ah, what mistake have I done?' He said, 'Ah, can I see your notebook?'

Then I took it, I gave it to him. He took it. I did not know that he was reading my name. (*Laughs.*)

Then he wrote my name and my surname. He gave it back to me. Then time came, we all went out. They said, 'Oh, school is over now, we are going home.' So we all went our way.

And as we went, all the boarders together, we were running now, getting home. Then he sent someone saying, 'You go and give this letter to this girl.' And that fellow followed us. He was coming from far, but this one was coming very much closer to us. Then he called my name.

This is the boy now?

This was the young man whom he had sent. He said, 'I want to see so-and-so. I've got a letter for you.' Then the big girls looked back. They said, 'Ah. You see? It's a son of a reverend. He comes behind there. I think he's the one who has given him this letter. Let's run! Don't take it.'

So you ran?

I ran with the big girls. So that boy said, ' Ah, *iwe*, don't run away! Come and get your letter.' (*Laughs.*)

And you were still running?

I was still running. The big girls were encouraging me, 'You, run! Don't. You see, he's a son of a reverend. Come on, run!'

As I was running, I went a little bit farther, then a thought came, 'Ah, but why should I not get my letter? It's my letter. Let me see.' Then I went back, collected my letter. 'Ha! You have got that letter?' Oh. Not knowing that the big girls, I'm sure they were saying, 'Ah, we have been here all these years, how come he has written to you?' (*Laughs.*) 'What has he written to you?'

So then I read the letter. I kept quiet. I would say that he was now offering a proposal, saying, 'I love you' and so on, blah blah, all the love language. (*Laughs.*)

All the love language.

So I said, 'Hmm.' Then I had to reply. I said, 'Mmm, me, I am here for school. And if my father hears it at home he is going to withdraw me (*laughs*) from school.' He would not like to hear that someone is asking me for marriage.

Then I gave it back the following day...through the same boy. He writes back, says, 'Ah, me too, my brother is not yet married, you know that. I just want this to remain between you and me. Cos my big brother is not yet married, so I don't want anybody to know.'

Aaah! I tell you, that very week the news was out! (*Laughs.*) Then the following week, off he goes to school, the news remained.

By the way, were the letters in English or Tumbuka?

He was writing to me in English; I couldn't write in English at that time. I was only in Standard One and I'd been there for only two weeks!

Oh, soon after your arrival.

Mmm, hmm. And that really put me into such an awkward situation, that I was not very free now. I was so shy.

Especially since now they knew.

They knew. I felt very uncomfortable. But then that's how it started. Then he went to Blantyre Secondary School, kept on writing me. So during the holidays was when he came back. He wanted to see me. He first of all came straight to the boarding, asked for me from our mistress, this relation of mine. So, then they said, 'He wants to see you.' So then I went out with a friend. We went behind the school where we used to play football. There we chatted, chatted, then we came back. Not knowing that the white mistress had come. She came before I got there. I don't know what she wanted. Then she saw...because when she was coming from her house, her toilet was outside, so I think she saw us, 'Who are those people down there?'

Then from that time, she went and confronted our assistant mistress, 'Who are the girls that are there? Why are they there?' She couldn't explain much, but she had to. So our mistress said, 'When they come back, I want to see them.'

So after that, we went to see her. She called me, said, 'Why were you there?' and so on... So I said, 'This man came to the boarding and I had informed our assistant mistress.' She wasn't happy. She scolded me, then we went back.

So from that time, when he came again he wanted to see me, our assistant couldn't agree, she said, 'Because of these reasons.'

So my fiancé went and met this European lady. He said, 'I want to see my girlfriend.'

So then she told him, 'No, I don't agree that men should be coming here to disturb the girls.'

So whatever they discussed there, I don't know. Then he went away without seeing me.

After a week, he came back. They talked and talked, then eventually they came to see me. Then he went back to his school, so each time he came, he had to see her first before he could come to see me. He had to get permission from her.

So that's how we lived. Went on. Although I told our mistress, 'There's nothing, he just wants to see me.' But I think their way of life *kwawoko*, it was different. But then that was it, that's how it started.

But it was strange indeed. It was... I think it's true that sometimes marriage is arranged by God, that...you are going to live together. Because the time that he came to teach us, when I saw him, I just fell in love. Before he asked me. (*Laughs.*) I said, 'Ah, this man.' After so many had tried, because even right back at my home village, they started coming, looking for me, when I was twelve. And my mother would chase them right from the house, say, 'Ah, she's just a baby, what do you want, you people?' and I would cry. I had no time for anybody. And I never accepted anybody in my life, except this man. Honestly. So it was real love.

He used to call me his rose during courtship, and that's where the name Rose came from. Before that, I had also chosen a different name for myself: Tryness. I used it briefly, but later on started using the name Rose.

Do you remember the qualities that you liked, the qualities that may have made you fall in love with him?

Uhm...I should say, not really, sort of, the qualities of a person. But I don't know, I just saw him, I just loved him. When I met him, I saw him face to face, he came to teach us, it was really love at the glance. Even if he didn't ask me, I would still have admired him as, 'Ah, this man is a nice man,' (*laughs*), a nice-looking man.

He only taught for that one day?

One day. That was all. So that's why I thought, I said, 'Ah, as if it was an arrangement with his brother, 'Go and teach in that class and see if there are any girls that you would love.' (*Laughs.*)

You never asked him afterwards?

No. I didn't. I didn't ask him really, which I should have.

So your courtship mainly involved him coming to visit you at the school, then going.

Yes. For a long time we just courted like that, until when I was in Standard Four, then he came to our village during our holidays. He came to the village with his friend, because in those days with us here, if a man wants to come and see you, even if you have already agreed, he should not come alone, he should come with a friend. Only then did he come to see us at home and so on.

And what was his friend's name?

It was his nephew actually, Yuse Soko, a son of his sister.

They came to see us at Kafukule from Ekwendeni. That was the first time they came to see us.

So before all this, no-one knew that there was...

After all this, I think wind had reached home. So when he came to see us, they had known. Then his father died before the normal situation was done. I was in Standard Four when he came and went back.

It was then that they arranged to send *ankhoswe*; it was the time they had to send *mathenga* to approach my parents. And after that, everything was sorted out. But then I still went for my Standard Five. So while I was in Standard Five, while we were doing our Standard Five, my friend still continued teaching.

Now people were nagging us, 'Ah, you are grown up. When are you going to marry?' and so on. So after my Standard Five, then he said, 'I think it's high time we got married.' (*Laughs.*)

Portrait of a Father-in-Law

Rose Chibambo refers to her late father-in-law as a man who took good care of Livingstonia Mission and was respected by many members in the community.

Yesaya Chibambo, who died before the wedding of his son to Rose, was held in high esteem by the community because of his position as a reverend and his interest in Ngoni history. He wrote two books on the Ngoni: *My Ngoni of Nyasaland* (1942) and *Midauko: Makani gha ba Ngoni* (published posthumously in 1961). He worked as a teacher before becoming a reverend, and was the first recipient of the Honours Diploma for Schoolmasters in Nyasaland in 1920.[i]

He was also one of the few Africans to write to the leaders of the Livingstonia Mission about the inequalities in the treatment of African and European missionaries. Below is an excerpt of his letter, written in 1921:

> There is a great fear on the part of the native to write to the masters or officials, and such fear conceals much of his thought from the mind of the European. I know that if a child has fear towards a father, simply because of incurring some punishment, that child does not really understand the mind of his father. [...]
>
> When are Natives to be included in the Mission staff? Because one sees that a native has no voice in the mission work. There are several reasons to be laid down under this question:
>
> 1. The native is not regarded as a co-worker with the missionary.
>
> 2. The native worker is commonly called 'boy' by his missionary without any distinction.
>
> 3. The native does not see the way to believe that the work on which he is placed is his, and that with his aid, he will enable his missionary and master, to bring up indigenously the growth of his native country, to an intellectual and spiritual ability, for serving God and man; but by threats he works with fear.
>
> 4. One sees that he is slightly esteemed, so is his work.
>
> 5. No native is allowed to report about his own work...[ii]

Kenneth Ross reports that while the Mission Council 'made some attempt to show understanding,' it was clear that they were not willing to address Chibambo's concerns or change the way in which they ran the Mission.[iii] The Mission even went as far as to say that Chibambo's assertion that African teachers and others were not considered co-workers was 'made without thought and is not true.'[iv] Interestingly, long after the letter had been written and his father had died, Edwin Chibambo would resign as a teacher because of the inequalities that he saw in the teaching profession.

Chapter 9

Wedding Preparations and Marriage

1940s

WEDDING AND MARRIAGE

Eh, I tell you. In our tradition at that time, when a child was getting married...

This day came. People had to come into my mother's house. My father was there, my mother was there. Then families had to come, husband and wife, my aunties. *Agogo* had died at that time. So then they call you into the house, either with your sister-in-law, or with your aunt. Imagine it: all these elderly that are there, they are now giving advice. Because with us, you have to move from your village; you are now going to the man's village.

Now because Ekwendeni was far, and this was now in the morning hours, they had all to put in their words, 'You are no longer going to be with us here. You are moving away from our village, going to a new village, to go and stay with people that you have never known.'

And then, they encourage you to be on your best behaviour: 'If you behave well, you are going to find it easy to get on with people.' And usually, they tell us that whatever they do in that house, learn from your mother-in-law, and that's what you should also do. 'Whatever we do here, leave things here. But follow what those people are doing at their village. Unless if they are witches, then you can run away, because that we don't do here. But apart from that, you have to listen to your mother-in-law, whatever she guides you.'

Then after that, when you come out of that house, we used to go into a *kraal*, where all the cows stay. Because when they had proposed marriage, they had to pay a dowry. So that dowry was in the form of cows. They were put in that *kraal*. So they would take me into that *kraal*. In that *kraal* now, we make a circle with all the elderly people, and a few of my girls, my girlfriends. Then we have a song, which we sing in Ngoni, especially for that day. (*Laughs.*)

I've forgotten the song. We sing and dance in a very polite manner. When you are going, you also have to take a cow. I must go with a cow, which must be slaughtered on the wedding day at the man's home. It must be used as *ndiwo* on that wedding day *uko*. My husband-to-be will also produce a cow, if they are children from the well-to-do families.

But if they are not, they can't do it. But if they are not, what they carry, they carry... what would I say...the droppings of a cow. They will take the dry droppings to say that this is what we have brought. So, wherever you go they know that they have no cow, and this is what they have brought.

But I had to take a real cow. And then they say, 'you first of all have to hit it. You hit it'. and show it the way. So I hit it, and then it had to go out through the door, following the way, where I'm going to go. So as I hit it, then I followed it behind. So it went, and I kept on following it. And I'm told, 'Don't look behind. Just follow it.' And that's what I did.

So it's you and your girlfriends and the cow.

Yes. We go. Then...you hit it, and it just went out. And you follow it behind. So you have young men, and an elderly man, to make sure that it follows its way. So then you just follow behind, then the elderly sing, and you can't stop crying. Oh, you really cry. You cry that you have left your parents and your village. So then you go.

So, being far, we walk a long distance. We reach there at night. When you get there, we are now outside, then they know that the people have come because of the cow, which will go in first with those people.

Then they will also sing their song, and of course they say, 'Ho-ho! Ho-ho!' (*Laughs.*) These are now people from your home, telling them that here we are. We have come.

So then they go right in the *kraal*. Then you and all the crowd that you have brought, they also go with you. And they carry all your belongings that you have brought, which you will use in your home. You carry flour, you carry... If you are really a child from a well-to-do family, they will have killed a cow for you before you came and dried it, and then they have carried it in big pots. Now they carry maize meal and so on, beans, groundnuts, already pounded, cos they expect that you cannot go out pounding and so on. So that's it.

I wore a white dress with a veil. It's unfortunate in those days, it was very difficult to find photographers. But we had a photograph much later and unfortunately, the man who photographed us was from Tanzania and he didn't give us our photo. We haven't seen our photo.

I had one which one of the missionaries took, but I don't know. Ah, I don't know where it went, especially during the Crisis, when we were...no, during the State of Emergency, when they were just scattering everything that we had; it's when a lot of things got lost.

How you would you describe the early years of marriage?

It was beautiful... it was very beautiful. We never quarrelled. Yes, we may disagree on something, but never quarrelled with my late husband. It never happened. No. If there were conflicts, they may have come from outside, but not between us. No. Even those from outside would only just make us—both of us—miserable. But not that one of us would be influenced by it.

You have already described to me the situation in your village, how there were very close networks. When you went to your new home, was it the same that you had another extended kind of network?

At the Chibambos', it was also a Ngoni family. It was the same. As families, we were close. In fact, after my people had gone, then...your in-laws will have to spread a mat somewhere...they take you out of the house, they will make you sit there, a few elderly will sit there, they are also welcoming you, and they are also telling you the type of life where you have come to. They say, 'This is your mother-in-law, you have to take care of her; the fact that she is a mother-in-law means that she's an old person now, and you are the one who is to take care of her.'

But I was a third daughter-in-law, so that they had to say, 'Well, you have your sisters-in-marriage, but you have to do your part, too.' And then, they tell you that you have to respect all the elderly people here and you have to cook. 'Remember to share out the food to the old people.'

So after that, they actually will take you to a place...to a kitchen, put the food there...the pot there...and they give you the number of plates where you will have to *gawa nsima* and to which people: 'This plate will go to so-and-so, this one will go to so-and-so.' So then they say, 'Here it is. You cook.'

At first, they help you to cook. You cook with them. Then...you *gawa nsima* in the plates like they have told you, and you dish out the relish and everything. Then, let it go. And where it goes, it's to the old people. So, at the time I came, there were two elderly people, so I had to take the food to them. And then to mother-in-law, and then to the brother-in-law, who was now like the father-in-law. That's it.

And then they gave me a girl. They said, 'This is the child which we will give you...you will look after her, and she's the one whom you will be sending for whatever you want to do.' That's how it was. It was nice.

So meanwhile your husband was teaching, too?

At the meantime, when this was being done, he was there at home. Then, with us, after that, time came that he had to go for teaching. So we left together to go to Livingstonia where he was teaching, and together with this little girl too; she was Dorothy. Dorothy Chibambo. She died only about three weeks ago [in 2012].

I know what you said about how it was not about the qualities that attracted you to your husband, but all the same, how would you describe him?

One thing, he was a man whom I had not known. The first time he came into the class, that was my first time to see him and that was his first time to see me too. But my husband was a quiet person.

If someone was to compare the two of you, who would they say was more outgoing?

(*Laughs.*) Perhaps I was. I say so because sometimes, in most cases, when visitors came into the house, my husband would be there, he would greet them and find out how they are and so on, it ends there. (*Laughs.*) He had nothing to talk about with them anymore. Unless they started talking politics. Otherwise he had nothing to talk about with them. So anytime I came home I will say, 'Ah ah, this house is so quiet. What is going on?' (*Laughs.*)

I have six children. One boy, the first-born, and five girls. The first born is Roy Yesaya, then there is Royce Elizabeth. Apart from the name Roy, the names were given by my mother-in-law. After Royce, there is Malibase, then Khataza. The fifth-born had several names. She was given the name Mkaidi by the friends I had in prison, since I took her with me to prison when I was arrested. Mkaidi means prisoner. Later on, we called her Gadi, again in reference to prison. The former president Dr Hastings Kamuzu Banda named her Mtamayani, after his sister, who looked after him. Gadi's other name is Mhlabase. The sixth-born is Phumile Kusile, names also given by my mother-in-law. Her other name was Kwacha. Phumile was born after we had come out of prison.

And the name Roy, did it have anything to do Roy Welensky?

No, there were no links with Roy Welensky. The name was given by missionaries.

Teary Wedding Songs

Rose Chibambo explains the reason she cried on her wedding day, an otherwise festive occasion: she was leaving her parents and her village.

If one listened to the songs performed during a typical Ngoni wedding at the time, the message would have, perhaps, justified some tears. Read's collection of wedding songs highlights those that were performed during *umsindo* and *mthimba*. Although not all of the songs were sombre, there were still those which focused on loss and death. Apart from the songs admonishing the bride-to-be against jealousy, there were songs which referred to the girl as someone who was about to be killed. As in the following translation by Read:

> We say who will be killed this year?
>
> Thou chosen one open the fort for us.
>
> Let us enter
>
> We say who will be killed this year?[i]

The idea of an open fort suggests the family's sense of vulnerability as the girl is taken away to her prospective husband's village.

Another example is the following song that was supposed to be sung by the bride:

> I am a stray, a stray
>
> Behold my father has given me up
>
> I shall wonder (*sic*) to the wild country
>
> My father has given me up.[ii]

Such songs, with their emphasis on the girl's departure, would have brought home to the bride-to-be a sense of foreboding. She would have to get used to a new family, quite often far from home.

Chibambo was fortunate in that she took a cow with her to the in-laws. But as her narrative shows, there were those who did not have cows. The song below may have been painful to hear for brides who had brought cows, but it must have stung when the bride-to-be did not have a cow:

Thou child of a wanderer, thou art mine.

Though child without a father, thou art mine.

Hoya yi yoya

Thou who bringest a present like a house rat because thou hast no cattle

I have now brought a present to my comrades.[iii]

With such epithets as 'child of a wanderer,' 'orphan,' and 'daughter of a madman,' the bride-to-be would have been keenly aware that the familiar structures that had shaped her world were no longer there. When one considers that for the men, the songs did not focus on the sense of alienation, then perhaps it is not surprising that some brides felt a sense of loss, even though these were not forced or arranged marriages.

Chapter 10

Moving into Political Spaces
1950s

How did you get involved in politics?

I was a bit curious. It was the time when Federation had started. It was at its height, I must say, because the discussion of Federation started years back.

So at that time, I was then living in Zomba, at Mapale Lines. Then, I was just used to the fact that I never ate food alone, without my husband. Each time I cooked, I knew he was at work, but I knew when he would be back. I would cook, put food on the table, and wait for him to come. So he would come, then we would have food together. All the time.

But when this politics intensified, my husband now started coming late, late. So one of the days I said, 'What is it that is keeping you away?' Not that I had a feeling that perhaps there is somebody somewhere, no, because I trusted him.

So he said, 'Oh, I'm sorry I didn't explain to you. I come late because as soon as we knock off, then we get together with friends, start talking about politics. You know this country is actually being taken up by the whites.' He said, 'The settlers want to federate this country. Northern Rhodesia, Southern Rhodesia and Nyasaland. They want them to be in one Federation, one country as a federal country.'

So I said, 'Ah. How?'

He said, 'Well, this is what they want, so that they will rule us. We will not be able to rule ourselves. They will continue ruling us under Federation.'

So I said, 'No. How can that be?'

He said, 'Yes, this is what it is. So in most cases I spend time there, we discuss with friends and so on.'

So I said, 'Wherever you meet...er...do women attend those meetings?'

He said, 'No. So far I have never seen any woman attending that meeting.'

'Mmm. Can I attend the meetings?'

He said, 'Oh, you're free. You're free; you can come. You can attend the meeting and hear what goes on.'

So I said, 'I see.'

Then after some days, I said, 'Can I invite my friends to come with me?'

By then you had not gone yet?

No, I had not gone. He said, 'You can bring your friends, it doesn't matter, you will be welcome.'

So from that time, I felt that I should organise some of my friends, so that when we went, we would go together.

It happened that the following day, I went to the hospital. And as I was coming from hospital, going to Mapale, there is a recreation hall—you have been to Zomba— there is a recreation hall. As we used to walk from hospital, or from Mapale going to the hospital, we used to pass through the recreation hall.

Is this what they call Zomba Community Hall?

It's the same one. At that time we used to call it Recreation Hall. So then, having gone to the hospital, on my way back, as I was coming, I found that the hall was crowded with chiefs, all the chiefs from Southern Region, they were there.

But then I wondered, I said, 'Ah, what is going on here?'

They were being addressed by...somebody at that time whom they called Relations Officer...African... It was somebody who was responsible for the African affairs in the government of that time, and he was a white man.

So he had gathered these chiefs in order to explain to them how good Federation was. So as I was coming, they were having a break, and they were on the veranda.

I identified one chief; this was Chief Chikowi. Then I went closer to him, I said, 'Ah, what is going on here?' He said, '*Ah, si za akazi zimenezi. Chokani. Mulibe nazo ntchito, si za akazi iyayi.*' ('This is not for women. Leave. This is none of your business. It is not for women.')

I said, 'Ah. But I'm asking, what is going on?'

He said, '*Aah. Tiyeni uko. Si za akazi.*' ('Go away. This is not for women.')

So other chiefs were coming near to him. Then he says, 'Eh, let's go in, they are going to pelt us with stones. Let's go in.'

They were all now walking in. Then while he was there, before he went off, I became so

Above: Chibambo's paternal ancestors, the Ngoni. Here, Angoni warriors in Zomba at the coronation celebrations for King George V, 1911 (Society of Malawi, Historical and Scientific)

Below: Women pounding maize, undated. A common duty for many women in Malawi, explained by Chibambo in Chapter Five (Society of Malawi, Historical and Scientific)

Above: Shoes as markers of racial difference, shoes as a privilege for white missionaries only. The Wedding of Lewis and Grace Bandawe at St. Michaels Church, 31 May 1913 (Society of Malawi, Historical and Scientific)

Below: An example of a Malawian village, ca. 1960 (Society of Malawi, Historical and Scientific)

emotional. I said, 'You are busy selling our country down the river.' And I was crying. Then he says to the others, 'Let's go in,' so they went away into the hall.

But I felt so bad; I was literally crying. Then from there, I walked away, going to my house in Mapale. I got there, then in the evening I explained to my husband what had happened. So he said, 'Yes, this is what is going on. This government, they are getting all our chiefs and they are trying to influence them, telling them how good federation is, and how important they will be, and that they will be very rich when this country gets federated. Which is not true, so they are cheating them.'

I said, 'Right. Now I'm on the mission.'

Then I started going to speak to my friends with my baby on my back.

You only had one child at the time?

At that time I had two. Him Roy and the second one Royce. So then I went talking to my friends within Mapale. Going from house to house, and I used to do that when their husbands were back from work, so that I should speak to them in the presence of their husbands, in case they might think that I'm trying to draw them to something which is dangerous. At least the husband too should hear.

Then I went, talking to my friends, from house to house. I said, 'You see, there is this federation, which is coming. They are going to federate our countries: Northern Rhodesia, Southern Rhodesia and Nyasaland. Now you know how much our people are suffering in South Africa. They are digging in the mines, some of them die, others come. Although they come, they come with empty suitcases, without anything, and those are the children whose mothers we are. We have to do something, and the men are meeting. What should we do?'

They would say, '*Ah. Iwetu ndiye ukuziziwa. Nanga ife taziziwa?*' ('You are the one who knows these things. Do we know these things?')

'Yes, let us get on with it.'

Then I went round, talking to everyone from house to house, literally. Now they agreed with me. They said, 'Yes.'

So I said, 'Alright. Now, let us call up a meeting.'

We called a meeting. Before we went to join the men, I said I should organise my fellow women. So we went in the same hall where the chiefs had been, we also went in there.

We had our meeting. So we discussed and we agreed. I said, 'Now, we should have elections.'

Even now, today, I just wonder how things were flowing. So they said, 'Yes, let us have an election. How does it go?' You know, in those days, they were ordinary mothers. They had never attended something like a meeting before.

So I said, 'Now what we should do is to elect a chairman,[8] a secretary and a treasurer. The little money we might be getting, contributing in order to buy paper that we should be writing on, we have to have a treasurer. '

They said, 'Fine.' Then we chose leaders.

So they said, 'Ah-ah. The chairman, you have to be the chairman. Because none of us know this thing. So you're the one to chair.'

For the position of secretary, we chose Mrs Kachingwe, NyaNkhata, from Kasungu. Then treasurer, we chose Mrs Chibambo, aNyaPhiri, my sister-in-marriage. She was a senior, she was married to Qabaniso, the eldest brother of my late husband. And her husband was actually the one, after all that—he was the one who was exiled in Port Herald. They had put him in exile because they said he's spoiling others because of politics. He used to go at night, visiting chiefs with his friends, talking to the chiefs, and he was an interpreter of a district commissioner. But the women chose the wife, they said, 'Ah, she can be a treasurer.'

Then after that, we said, 'Fine, these are the elections now. These are our leaders. What we should do now, we need to draw a constitution.'

Where ideas were coming from, I cannot tell you now. But when I look back, how things were flowing, I just don't know. I said, 'Well, now we have to draw a constitution for our body. What should we call it? Oh, let us call it Nyasaland African Congress, Women's League.' That's how we called it Nyasaland African Congress, Women's League.

So then they said, 'Fine.' And I drafted a constitution, put it in writing, just on a very plain paper. We had nobody to type it for us. At that time we said, 'Still it is written, one can read it.'

I wrote it and I took it to the District Office.

So you wrote this constitution?

---

[8] For a long time, the word 'Chairman' was used in Malawi for both men and women in leadership positions. This was because of the assumption that leaders were often male.

I wrote the constitution, and I took it to the DC's office to have it registered. So there they pushed me to a lady who was dealing with social welfare. There was Miss Smith. Then I gave it to her.

She was typical Nyanja, Catherine Smith. Her father was a missionary in Ntcheu. So she grew up there and she spoke fluent Nyanja. 'Ah, what is this that you have brought?' So I said, 'This is a constitution of our league, which we have formed.'

She read it through. 'Eh! So this is the thing you want to run?'

I said, 'Yes.' Then they accepted it. They took it. I said, 'That's it.' We went ahead. Then I called for another meeting to come and explain to them that it has now been registered. Now we can go ahead.

That's how it started. That was now the beginning, in 1952.

There was a lot that we did as the Women's League in Zomba. One major incident: the women were complaining about the hospital, the antenatal clinic. We used to go to the antenatal clinic and would have only one screen…no…not even a screen to hide, but they would put up beds, sometimes three to four beds, where women would be going to be examined. So sometimes about four people, you are lying there, and then you are being examined while others are seated here, watching. And that really disturbed women, but they had no way of saying anything.

So we made an appointment to see the…that time we had the Director of Health. So we made an appointment with him. We went to see him. And we said, 'There's this thing which has been going on at the hospital, at the antenatal clinic, where we are being examined. Some are just beginning now and they are watching their older mothers being examined. This is not on in our tradition.' And we talked. It caused an uproar at the hospital. So then that time, I became very unpopular (*laughs*) with the hospital, but I didn't mind.

Then there was the issue of the colour bar. As I had said to the women, 'You know the troubles we have here. This is the beginning of Federation. We cannot go into Mandala shop and buy things. They send us to a window. You cannot enter the shop because you are black.'

And indeed, there was a window. If I wanted to buy anything, they would say, 'You go and stand by the window', and I used to refuse. I said, 'I'm not going to go at a window. How am I going to choose what I want?'

Then the saleslady would send my own brothers who were their watchmen there, *wosesa*, 'Chase her out.' Then they would come, be pushing us out, '*Nonono, simuyenera kulowa muno.*' ('You're not supposed to enter this shop.') Yes, it used to happen. '*Musalowe muno iyayi. Simolowa anthu akuda. Kayimeni apo pawindo.*' ('Don't enter this shop. Africans are not supposed to be in here. Go and stand at that window over there.') Oh yes. These things were there. You can't enter Mandala, you cannot enter Kandodo.

If at all we want to buy anything that we cannot find in the Indian shop, you have to go and stand by the window. And you will be talking to that person, *wosesa, ndiye uziti 'ah, mundionereko chakuti'* (you would tell the sweeper, 'please check if the shop has this or that'). So it was a typical colour bar. And I said, 'All these things are happening, what more if we get into Federation with those people in Southern Rhodesia? And those in South Africa? Boers and the way they treat our people. This is how they want us to be treated.'

The women were up in arms. So that was the beginning of our Women's League.

After a while, then they transferred me from Zomba to Blantyre. (*Laughs.*) Transferred my husband, my husband was transferred now to Blantyre. So I felt that, 'Oh, perhaps they said, let her get away from here.' At that time, my husband had stopped teaching at Livingstonia Mission. As soon as we got married actually, he only taught for a few months. The first term with me, that was the first and the last. I think he disagreed with the missionaries, felt that he was now a family man, and they were not paying him enough. And in any case, at that time, he was the only English Grade teacher, but then because he was a young man, they said, 'Ah, no. We can't pay him all that money. There are old people here.' So those people that were senior, then, you know, they used to talk to them, 'Ah, you see,' the missionaries would talk to them, 'You see, this young man wants to be paid more than you.' So he felt very unpopular, so he said, 'I'm not coming anymore.' Then he left, and he went and joined the civil service. That's how we ended up being in Zomba. Yes, and he joined the civil service, the PWD, Public Works Department.

So after our transfer we ended up in Blantyre. Now the Zomba group didn't continue as much...the chair was gone. But when I got to Blantyre, I joined the main body, Nyasaland African Congress, because they had heard of my interest. So this was the time now, the time we started our Women's League, in 1952, in December, we organised it. And then when I got to Blantyre, 1953 in March, people knew by then I was interested in politics, so each time the Blantyre branch was calling its meeting, we used to attend the NAC meetings.

You and your husband?

Yes. Then they called up a meeting....elections rather. They called for an election in

Blantyre. So during the elections for the district, Mikeka Mkandawire was the chairman, and he was a very influential man, and Hartwell Solomon was the secretary, he was from Chiradzulu. And I was elected the treasurer.

A number of people were surprised, some even came to the house to congratulate me. It was strange to them that a woman should be elected into the main body. They would say, 'Ah, *akusankhani bwanji inu? Ndiye mwaloladi?*' ('How did they choose you? And you've accepted?') I said, 'Yes, I'm happy to be there.'

So then we carried on politics in the main branch. But at the meantime, I said, 'No. Something must be done.' Others would hear that there's a lady who's a treasurer and so on, she attends meetings, but when I was now familiar with Blantyre, and I knew some families and so on, I started, again, going to meet them in person.

I went, I met Mrs Katunga, at that time she was née Kahumbe. I met Mrs Mlanga—Margaret Mlanga—talked to her, I went to talk to Mrs Chikafa. Then after meeting them, I said, 'Why can't we be having our own meetings? You should have the interest to come too, to attend even men's meetings.'

So after talking to them, they got convinced that it was worth getting together. But *osalephera mantha* (fear was inevitable). I said, 'No. There's nothing, let us just carry on.' So we started the meetings. Then we had an election, called up the women, we had an election.

I was still called to be chairman.

Now this was the Women's League in Blantyre?

Women's League in Blantyre now. Then I was made the chairman, Mrs Mlanga was made secretary, Mrs Katunga was the deputy secretary, and Mrs Chikafa was the treasurer. Then through these friends, we tried to influence a number of people coming in.

We kept on going. Now, the main body. At that time, things were hot. Manoah Chirwa was teaching at HHI. Afterwards, he was dismissed cos they said he's influencing the students. Then when we started this in Zomba, when the Women's League was born, that time, even when we came to Blantyre, at that time, the chairman, president of the main body, the Nyasaland African Congress, was James Chinyama. Now, the men, they were very strong.

Now later on, James Chinyama retired. Then it was Mr Sangala who came up to be the chairman. Then at one time, the main body under Mr Sangala as a president called for a public meeting at Ndirande. This was in 1956. The people went, and they addressed the meeting. As a result, he was arrested, together with his secretary. They said he was inciting the people to rise against the government. So on the day that the case was to be held in Zomba, we, the women, hired a bus from Blantyre, full of women, went to Zomba and we sang, going round the whole court. When we came to Zomba, now the Zomba women joined us.

We kept on singing and singing, until they just gave them a fine instead of sending them to prison.

What kind of songs were you singing?

Nkhondo, nkhondo, nkhondo, lero,
Sitifuna nkhondo
Nkhondo, nkhondo, nkhondo lero
Sitifuna nkhondo.
Sitifuna, sitifuna Welensike, tikufuna
Boma lathu.

(War: We don't want war
We don't want Welensky
We want self-government.)

And we kept on singing, *sitifuna chitaganya, tikufuna boma lathu* (we don't want federation, we want self-government). And we sang, going around the court. I think they saw that mmm, things here are not so good. Instead of locking them up they said, 'We are charging you, you have to pay a fine of so much.'

The money was contributed there and then. It was paid off, and they were released. And it was really hurrah. That was when we packed ourselves again in the bus which we had hired. We went back to Blantyre.

After having marched.

Yes. Yes. Marching round the High Court. Singing. (*Laughs.*) These are the powers of women. Then men get encouraged. (*Laughs.*) So then we went back to Blantyre, we went back to our usual politicking.

That's how politics of the women started. We never used to look forward to any compensation from anybody or for a reward from anybody. Our aim was to see that our country is free. It is ruled by a black man. So that we have to have the real freedom that we can have. This was the main aim that we had. And we carried on until the whole country was convinced, all the women had joined in every branch in the country, had joined politics. They were joining the main body, at the same time they were now organising themselves. We had no transport but whenever there is a main body meeting and the delegates are coming from areas, they would see that the women are doing this. It was encouraging. That's how the Women's League started.

The Federation of Rhodesia and Nyasaland, 1953

Famously called 'the stupid federation' in several speeches by Malawi's first president, Dr Hastings Kamuzu Banda, the Federation of Rhodesia and Nyasaland officially commenced on 1 August 1953 and would last for a decade. Owen Kalinga points out that despite starting in 1953, plans to rule the three countries as a federation had already been underway decades earlier.[i] The idea behind federation was to favour white minority rule in Northern Rhodesia (present-day Zambia), Southern Rhodesia (present-day Zimbabwe) and Nyasaland (present-day Malawi). The Federation was thus to the advantage of settlers in the three territories. As early as 1935, government heads of Nyasaland and the Rhodesias had met in order to discuss a partnership in matters of trade and tariffs, education and defence. One of the implications of the Federation was that the territories would be governed by the Queen's representative. Although the initial agreement, in 1941, had been that the three territories would have a partnership which would be limited to non-political matters, the functions of the partnership had expanded by 1944[ii] to include the political aspect.

Chibambo makes reference to Roy Welensky when she talks about the protest song performed by women in the Nyasaland African Congress. Welensky, a British politician from Northern Rhodesia, was a strong advocate for the Federation. He would later become second and last prime minister of the Federation of Rhodesia and Nyasaland or Central African Federation (CAF), as it was sometimes called.

Kamuzu Banda opposed the Federation long before he came to Nyasaland. In 1949, he co-authored a memo with Northern Rhodesian Harry Nkumbula, warning that Federation would result in segregationist ideas, which were dominant in Southern Rhodesia. Among other notable figures who opposed the Federation were Edward K. Gondwe, Clement Kumbikano, Chief Mwase of Kasungu, Ellerton Mposa and Alexander Muwamba. In 1951, they were invited as Nyasaland delegates during a federation conference and refused to consider federation.[iii]

In contrast to such views, some chiefs at the time, such as Chitera, Kadewere and Ntondeze (and Chikowi, as noted in Chibambo's account), were seen by their subjects as being sympathetic to the ideas of Federation.[iv] In the colonial administration, Federation was justified as a move that would allow for a diversified economy of British Central Africa and would 'raise standards of living for the European colonialists, and greatly aid the social advancement of the African.'[v] Those who supported federation were also of the view that it would, in principle, encourage racial cooperation, and would be far much better than apartheid in South Africa.[vi] This view of a racial partnership was actually in the Federal Constitution, but as journalist Elias Mtepuka scathingly put it, '...lips which mouth "partnership" are betrayed by hands which manipulate apartheid,'[vii] a reference to the colour bar as it was practised in the three countries.

The pro-government newspaper at the time, the *Nyasaland Times*, clearly felt that you could really never be 'too' federal when they criticised the fact that the federal flag was not as prominent as they would have wanted:

> Why be shy about the Federal Flag?
>
> It appears that the Federal Government is the only one timid about flying its flag amid a profusion of others....[viii]

And on the same page, there was a commentary from the *Nyasaland Times*' mascot, the CAT:[9] 'Nyasaland may have been the Cinderella of the Federation once but she doesn't have to be shy today about her fairy Federal godmother.'[ix]

Back to the man at the Recreation Hall, Chief Chikowi. The chief's confrontation with Rose Chibambo was not the first with the family. McCracken[x] reports that McKinley Qabaniso Chibambo had been involved in attempt to overthrow Chikowi in 1953, an act which led to his exile in Port Herald until 1960. In 1959, he would be given an award on Queen Elizabeth II's birthday during what was known as the Federal Honours for his role in 'fighting congress.' According to the *Nyasaland Times*, Chikowi was given the award, and MBE (Member of the Most Excellent Order of the British Empire), because he had: 'Strong anti-Congress views despite threats. Refused any congress meetings in area and kept it free from trouble during disturbances.'[xi]

---

[9] The acronym CAT was a play on the words *Central African Times* as well as on the image of a cat, which was the paper's mascot.

Chapter 11

Out with the Old, in with the New
1950s

Time came when we gave a mandate to two of our members to join the Federal Government. These two members were Wellington Manoah Chirwa and Clement Kumbikano.

They went to the Federal Government with our mandate that whenever we said, 'There's nothing we are gaining from the Federal Government, you better come back. Make sure that you are going to come back,' they would do so.

This was the mandate that they had. At first, we wanted to boycott the Federal Assembly. But then we said, 'Even if we say no, we don't want Federation, and we are out here, still this government, this colonial government, will choose stooges, our fellow Africans, whom they will say are representing us. And they will go there, they will say nothing. Therefore let us choose our own people who are going to express our own views that we are against Federation.' That's how Manoah was chosen, and Kumbikano. And the mandate was that when time comes and we say, 'Leave, it's enough, you have told them,' they shall come back.

Unfortunately, when they left, it went on and on, and when they were told to come back, according to them, they thought that time was not ready yet, that they should come back: 'We still have a duty to perform here.' So we said, 'No. They have known that Nyasaland is against it.'

So, since they refused, that was it. Perhaps had Manoah come back to be with us, he could have been the president. Perhaps Dr Banda would not have been called. But because he refused, that was it.

Now vocal people at that time were the young people. There was, for instance, my brother-in-law, Qabaniso, whose wife had been the treasurer in Zomba. He had been convicted; they said he was a dangerous man against the Federation. So the colonial government at that time convicted him, and he was serving a fifteen-month sentence in Zomba. He was in prison. And when they released him from there, they sent him to Port Herald, in exile. It was a terrible situation for the family. We were affected, but we did not stop taking part in politics.

But from that time, civil servants were barred from doing politics. No civil servant was allowed to attend political meetings or to say anything on political views, because he's working for the government and he cannot speak politics against the government which he's working for.

So the country became almost paralysed. But then there were people like Mikeka Mkandawire. That Mikeka Mkandawire was a strong man. He still stood in the Blantyre District, and then, at that time, Chipembere had now come back from school and he was in local government. Kanyama Chiume also had come back from East Africa; he was then in the country. And then, at that time, as I said Manoah had been dismissed and he was now there. I think it was before Manoah went to Federal Assembly, when there came an election for the Legislative Council in Malawi. We felt that there was need to increase the number of Africans in the Legislative Council. I think there were only three; we wanted five.

Then the idea came that we must also choose our own people to stand. We had to influence the chiefs, because at that time, people who went to Legislative Council were only chosen by chiefs. Nobody else. Provinces had to choose.

So in the Northern Region, we were given one candidate. In the Southern Region, they were given two candidates and in the Central Region, I think they had one or two candidates. So then we said, 'No. Kanyama and Chipembere must join the Legislative Council, because they will then speak our views.'

So my husband and I had Kanyama literally come to approach us, saying, 'Please, you better help.' We had to write letters to chiefs.

We wrote letters to Chief M'belwa, Katumbi, to chiefs that we knew. We said, 'Please choose your own son. Kanyama is your own son and we know that he will speak the views for the good of our country. We need this country to be independent.' So then we had to write letters, we influenced Southern Region chiefs, even some of the Central Region, 'Please choose your own people.'

So that's how Chipembere was chosen and Kanyama was chosen to go to Legislative Council. Then when they were at Legislative Council, they were talking our views. Of course there were about five people, I think; Mr Chinyama and Chijozi were in it. Then in the Southern region, it was Chipembere and Kwenje, Mr Kwenje. So in the North, they gave us only one.

Then that went on. But the Women's League was still intact, working hard with the bodies. Now at that time, elections had taken place. After that case where Mr Sangala and his secretary general Mr TDT Banda were almost imprisoned, but then only fines were issued. So after that, Mr Sangala called a general meeting that a new leader had to be elected. He didn't want to stand anymore. Well, there's a time people get tired. So elections took place, and TDT Banda was elected as president of the party.

Mr Kamchunjulu was elected the secretary. Was it Kamchunjulu? I'm sure it was Kamchunjulu. But this man was a policeman before, and he said he had retired, but after a lot of things happened, he was still a policeman.

So then I was now in the Central Body in the executive as a leader of the women. We carried on. But as I said, when the time came that Manoah wanted to continue in the Federal Assembly, and TDT Banda, being president of our party, also agreed with him, then we found that he wasn't that much worthy of leadership. That is, TDT Banda.

I forgot, when we were holding those elections, Dunduzu had come. In 1954, Dunduzu came back;[10] he was actually deported from Southern Rhodesia back to Malawi. He came and joined us.

And then his brother, Yatuta Chisiza, came back from East Africa. Then the party—the Executive—was strong. The party had almost died, before the arrival of these people. Kanyama was there in the Legislative Council, but I think we elected him after they had arrived.

But now, when, after they had arrived, then we held elections. It's when Dunduzu was secretary general of the party, Chipembere was treasurer, and Kanyama was publicity secretary.

Now, while we were struggling on, we found that the party was now becoming weak. Although the country was still hot, we were lacking leadership, especially with the issue concerning TDT Banda, which I have already talked about.

So, it was then that a meeting was called in Ramsey Hall. The chiefs were called to come and attend our meeting, because at that time, we felt that we were all young people...and talking to chiefs, it was just like a play, to tell them that we are going to be independent in this country, (*laughs*) we want to rule ourselves. They looked at us, say, '*Wana awa angofuna chabe kutifunira mavuto.*' ('These children just want to create problems for us.')

So anyway, before that, we organised a delegation, while TDT was the president. Dunduzu was then the secretary general, Yatuta was the administrative secretary. Then we said, 'No'. We said, 'We'd better go and demand from our government that we want to rule ourselves. We want to have self-government.' TDT was still the president then, so we made a delegation to go and meet the governor.

---

[10] According to Owen JM Kalinga and Cynthia A Crosby, Dunduzu Chisiza returned in September 1956 (*Historical Dictionary of Malawi*, Maryland and Kent: Scarecrow Press, 2001, p. 90).

TDT Banda, Dunduzu, Yatuta, Chipembere, Kanyama and I, we were all part of that delegation. We went to meet the governor and they took it as a joke; they didn't believe it. We got there, and we made our demand, 'We want self-government, we are not just talking. We want self-government in Malawi; we cannot continue with you people as a colonial government. We don't want the British to rule us forever.'

So I'm saying this: I was there as the leader of the women. As I said that most of us, we were…we had the spirit, but we were too young to convince our chiefs that we meant business; we were going to rule this country. So it was then that we had called the public meeting in Ramsey Hall and invited the chiefs to come and attend the meetings. It was there that Manoah was asked to resign from Federal Government. He refused. And it was there that he lost his popularity.

TDT, having agreed with him, also lost popularity. It was there and then that a decision was taken that we must invite Dr Banda to come back home and lead us. We had already known that he was there. He was in touch and a calendar at one time was circulated in Malawi—in Nyasaland then—with his picture and with all the leaders of Africa: Jomo Kenyatta, Nkumbula[11] and so on. So it was known that Malawi has got a son who is grown up, to come and rule the country.

Then we kept on. And Dr Banda was called, and he came 6th of July 1958. He arrived. He was supposed to have arrived earlier but he didn't come, reasons best known to him…

We actually expected him to arrive on the 29th of June. He did not come, but we all went to Chileka airport, and the airport was full of people, and people were really organised.

There was a young man—he's an old man now—Katola Nyoni, he organised the small chaps, composed songs for the arrival of Kamuzu. It was something unheard of, and they sang. They sang songs. There were so many of us at the airport until the plane came. But Kamuzu was not there. It was so…somehow embarrassing and very disappointing. Then people had to disperse and we went away.

But we were still convinced that he would arrive on the 6th of July. Perhaps he wasn't sure that we meant it, so he had wanted to prove it. After seeing the crowd that was

---

[11] Chibambo here refers to two famous nationalists, Jomo Kenyatta and Harry Nkumbula, from Kenya and Northern Rhodesia respectively. Kenyatta, given the honorary title *mzee* (meaning 'elder'), would later become Kenya's first president. Nkumbula, like Kamuzu Banda, was well known for his opposition to the Federation of Rhodesia and Nyasaland. He was president of the Northern Rhodesia African Congress, which later became the African National Congress (not to be confused with the African National Congress in South Africa). Nkumbula's party later lost to Kenneth Kaunda's United Independent Party partly because of Nkumbula's close association with the United Federal Party, which was dominated by Europeans.

there, I think that encouraged him.

Then come 6th of July, he arrived, and we were all relieved. Then a lot of things went through. The elections came. In fact, before he arrived, he had written to me when he was in Ghana, after he had already been approached. He wrote me to say that he was very happy with the work that I was doing. I had not met him; he had never seen me. But he heard of the organisation that I was doing, influencing the people on political issues.

So he arrived, and that day at Chileka, what was your first impression of Dr Banda?

The first day, when I saw him, I had the impression that he was a good leader and he had come to sacrifice for the country of Malawi. And then when he came, we organised, we carried on.

He found me in the central committee of the party, but he was still given an opportunity to choose the people that he would work with. But he still had to inherit the same executive; he didn't know people. So there we were, and, him being a new man to the country, everywhere we had to organise meetings, all over, at different times, for him to go and address people. At the same time for the people to see and know him. The whole country. We did that. And indeed Malawi was really on fire, calling for secession from the Federation. That was July 1958. August, September, October, November, December. We were doing everything, travelling to different parts of the country.

From TDT Banda to Hastings Kamuzu Banda

Thamar Dillon Thomas Banda, more commonly known as TDT Banda, was the fifth president general of the Nyasaland African Congress, which had been founded in 1944 by Frederick James Sangala, Levi Ziliro Mumba and Isaac Lawrence. He became president general in 1957. It was during his time as party leader that the youth were rallied as Kwacha Boys/Kwacha Builders 'to mobilize support and spread awareness of the NAC.'[i]

During the controversy on whether Manoah Chirwa and Kumbikano should come back from the Federal Parliament, TDT Banda, like Sangala before him, initially adopted a lenient attitude, which was not supported by some of the radicals in the party, such as Masopera Gondwe, Hartwell Solomon and Mikeka Mkandawire. In fact, these three had left the party because they did not like the fact that Chirwa and Kumbikano were allowed to be party members and still serve in the Federal Parliament.[ii]

In 1957, TDT Banda decided to expel the two from the party, a move which was supported by some members, including Rose Chibambo, Masauko Chipembere, Kanyama Chiume and Dunduzu Chisiza. These had been among the group of members who were calling for the withdrawal of Chirwa and Kumbikano from Parliament. However, the move ended up displeasing moderates such as James Chinyama and ND Kwenje. According to Andrew Ross, the rift between moderates and radicals after the expulsion came as a surprise 'to the young men and the one young woman who was beginning to make her presence felt in the movement, Mrs Rose Chibambo.'[iii]

In addition, TDT Banda, who had led a delegation on constitutional reform when the new governor, Sir Robert Armitage, had arrived in town, had not impressed his younger colleagues. Ross reports that it was Dunduzu Chisiza, not even an office bearer in 1957, who ended up speaking on behalf of the group during the meeting with the governor. The "young Turks"—Chisiza, Chipembere and Chiume, who were in their twenties—gradually lost confidence in TDT Banda.

However, as McCracken, Power and Ross all point out, the young Congress members felt that their age was a liability as far as leading Congress was concerned. The young Turks[12] decided to contact Dr Hastings Kamuzu Banda, who had run a medical practice in England for a long time before moving to Kumasi in Ghana. Banda had kept regular correspondence with the party and had at one point been described as a 'Resident Representative.'[v]

---

[12] This term is used by several historians, such as Robert Rotberg, Joey Power and Andrew Ross, no doubt because of the parallels with those who led the fight for political reform in the Ottoman Empire. It is often used to refer to Dunduzu Chisiza, Masauko Chipembere, Kanyama Chiume and those who agreed with their views and were within the same age range.

Power recounts that TDT Banda was actually sent by Chipembere to invite Banda to come home during the Ghanaian independence celebrations. It would seem that at this point, TDT Banda was not aware that he was sending the invitation to his future successor. Banda was noncommittal at the time.[vi]

Chipembere then wrote to Banda, asking him to come and 'help in the work of leadership,' an invitation which was deliberately vague.[vii] Kamuzu insisted on something more precise, the presidency of the Nyasaland African Congress.[viii]

Chipembere agreed to this. It was at this point that, according to Ross and Power, the plotting against TDT Banda began. Ross points out that the young men decided to use a trip that TDT Banda had made to India to question him on a donation that the Congress had received to help fund the trip. TDT was unable to give an explanation and was subsequently suspended and later expelled from the party in 1958, the same year that Banda arrived in Nyasaland. According to Ross, the visit to India was an 'unforeseen opportunity to clear the way for Kamuzu.'[ix]

Power specifically singles out Chipembere and Chiume as the masterminds behind the plot and points out that the trip to India never even happened; TDT Banda had no passport. That, however, did not stop the young men from making the accusation about the misappropriation of funds.[x]

Matthews Phiri was made interim president and just a few months later, in August, Kamuzu Banda was made party president at a conference in Nkhata Bay, which was TDT Banda's home district. The Congress members paid for ousting TDT Banda: 80 per cent of Congress members in Nkhata Bay boycotted the function, and the delegates to the function did not have much luck in terms of food. According to Ross, they mostly found themselves depending on porridge.[xi]

Chapter 12

The Meeting in the Bush and Time in Prison

1950s

In January 1959, we had our meeting in the bush.[13] At the bush meeting, unfortunately, I was the only lady.

Why unfortunately?

(*Laughs.*) We carried on with that meeting. Yes, it was on 2nd of January, I remember. We called delegates from all over the country to come and attend it. Our aim was that we have talked enough, now we have to show muscle. Passive resistance. That's what we had in mind.

And how were you going to demonstrate this passive resistance?

We were going to demonstrate, either sometimes close down the road, cut down the trees to close the roads. (*Laughs.*)

So that's what you had in mind.

But then the colonial government of Nyasaland claimed that we wanted to kill people, whites and the Indians. Little did we know. But when we were in the bush, we took it as a very secretive meeting.

Not that we didn't want anybody to know; we knew that they would still know. We had no place where we could hold that meeting, because to hold a meeting at that time, you had to get permission. And the hall was not ours; you had to beg for it from the district commissioner. So we held our meeting just behind Colby Hall, near Kapeni there. We sat down, and then we had our meeting and dispersed.

But at the meantime, things were happening, even if we did not know it. All of a sudden,

---

[13] The meeting in the bush was a two-day conference held at Kanjedza Afforestation Project, in Limbe, after the executive of the Nyasaland African Congress had failed to secure a hall. As Chibambo has pointed out, Congress members had initially planned to hold the meeting at Ramsey Hall, but they were not given access. They later held the conference at Mikeka Hotel, but since the space was not adequate, they decided to hold the second day of the conference at the Project (the bush). Kamuzu Banda was not present at the meeting. Key members of the Nyasaland African Congress who organised the meeting were Rose Chibambo, Dunduzu Chisiza, Kanyama Chiume and Masauko Chipembere. In our interview, Chibambo gives the date of the meeting as 2 January 1959. However, most written sources state that the meeting was on 25 January 1959. The aim of the meeting was to plan what the party would do in the event of Kamuzu Banda's arrest. The plan was to sabotage government activities. The extent of the planned sabotage has been a point of debate in Malawi's history, and I have included some of the perspectives on the meeting at the end of this chapter. Suffice to say that news of the meeting caused a great deal of alarm in colonial administrative circles, leading to the State of Emergency of 3 March 1959 and to subsequent arrests of members of the Nyasaland African Congress (Paul Chiudza Banda and Gift Wasambo Kayira, "The 1959 State of Emergency in Nyasaland: Process and Political Implications," *The Society of Malawi Journal* 65, no. 2 (2012): 1–19).

we saw strange people appearing in our Blantyre town and in many other main towns. Soldiers, foreign security forces. Then some of our friends, especially the missionaries, whispered to us, 'The government is plotting to arrest all the leaders of the Nyasaland African Congress.' So then indeed on 3rd March, everybody was arrested.

They arrested...some people thought that when these arrests come, they would only arrest the real leaders. Little did they know that they would also be arrested. Because some of the people were taken by surprise; they thought they were safe.

They swept even those people who were dodging us as politicians. They didn't want to associate with us because of fear that the government might see them, or the security...or the detectives or the *basirikalis* as usual would know that they associate with politicians. But they still came to sweep them (*laughs*). I tell you, many of them were taken by surprise, 'Ah ah, me too?! I was afraid!'

So all that caution for nothing?

(*Laughs.*) They were all swept. Ended up in prison. I was not arrested on 3rd March because by then I was expecting a baby, and I think they were afraid of the uproar, *kwawo, kuti* oh they have arrested a pregnant woman and put her in prison.

But then it was a terrible situation. As I was outside, every time, the minute I just moved out, security forces would come, ransack the whole house, mixing *ufa*, tearing all the chairs, tearing up everything...the whole house, chaotic. And the children would be really scared. All my children have lived a life of being scared, frightened, and at that time they were young then. You come back you find, '*Kunabwera ziazungu, anabwera momuno*' ('Some fierce white people came, they came into the house'). Ah, everything just....mixed up.

After two weeks, then I saw people coming. They said they had seen James Kalua, who had also been arrested, but he had now been released. So people said, 'Why has he still been released when everybody is still in prison?' And people were really concerned, even those we had thought were stooges; they were concerned.

So, I being left alone outside, and people were just mobilising, 'What can we do? This man is here?'

Because all the leaders were now in prison?

They were all in prison. 'Where have you seen him?'

So even drivers of the government would come to say, 'We have actually seen him. We have carried him together with the soldiers.' Okay. What do I do?

One day, it was on a Wednesday, I had to leave Blantyre and went to Zomba by bus in the hope that I would meet him. And I went, we arrived in Zomba. I don't know how I came to know that he would be...I said I must go and find out from the police. So then I walked from Zomba market, down to the police camp. I got there. I went straight to the house of the sub-inspector. And everybody was just wondering but I said, 'I don't mind.' So I got to the house of the sub-inspector.

He said, 'Ah. What sends you here?'

This was a Malawian sub-inspector?

Yes. A Mr Kumwenda. I said, 'I am looking for Mr Kalua. Do you know where he is?'

He gave me a seat. Then he called, 'Mr Kalua, somebody is here to see you.' Then he came out and when James saw me, he was scared. Then we greeted each other.

I said, 'I've come to see you.' Then the inspector left us. So I said, 'How have you managed to come out, and you are here, living with the inspector of police?'

Then Kalua was scared. I said, 'You have to tell me how you came out.'

So he didn't hide. He said, 'Yes. I hope nobody's listening to us.' He told me that he came out, they persuaded him that since he had not grown up in Nyasaland but had come from East Africa, joined the politicians, 'But now you can see what has happened, those fellows are going to rot in prison. So if only you can agree to be our witness—be a witness of the state—we are going to release you.' He said, 'This is how they released me. And they say that if I give them all the information, they are going to fly me out, out of this country, back to East Africa.'

So I said, 'Oh, I see. So that being the case, are you sure that we were plotting to kill the whites and the Indians? Is this true?'

Said, 'No, I know it is fake. It's not true.'

I said, 'Now, what type of witness are you going to be?'

So he assured me, he said, 'No, under the circumstances, I have agreed to say what they want me to say. But the minute I get out of this country, I'm going to denounce it, and say that this I have done through force. Because I was forced and I was supposed...I was bought, that's how I have come to say this.'

I said, 'Right. This being the case, you must put it in writing to me.'

So he said, 'Ah, yes I know, I'm going to publicise it in the papers.'

I said, 'Yes, you're going out, but in the meantime, as you are talking to me, I want you to put it in writing, so that I can have it.'

He found it hard. He said, 'You know, you never know as you will come out of here, they are going to search you and if they find it, they are going to kill you.'

I said, 'No.'

He said, 'I know.'

I tried. The fellow refused to give me any paper. He said, 'In any case, anyway, I will give it to you at the bus stop when you are boarding the bus.'

After a long time spent trying to convince him to write the note, I had to leave. I left, I said, 'You will find me at the bus stop.'

'Fine.'

I got to the bus stop. I waited. The bus was leaving around five. I sat there, waiting for Kalua to come. He didn't come. And I could not go to Blantyre empty-handed.

I had to find a place to sleep that day. I slept in Zomba.

You said you were pregnant at the time you travelled to Zomba?

Heavily pregnant. Almost full-term. Early in the morning, I went back. Ah, now he was shocked. 'You've come back again. You're still here?'

I said, 'I'm still here. I can't go empty-handed.'

We talked and talked. I tried here and there, he said, 'No, I can't....alright, I will organise one. I will give it to you. You go to the bus.'

I went back to the bus. He-e! He never came. I waited. I was supposed to take the twelve o'clock one, he didn't come. I left it, it went. I still waited.

Now he came at four-thirty. He came at the bus station, and found me there.

Said, 'Ah, so you're not gone?"

I said, 'No, I can't go.'

And he said, 'Please, believe me. I cannot give it to you now. If I give it to you, I will be in trouble. '

In fact, this second day, when I went there to talk to him, the inspector—sub-inspector—he came and called him, he said, 'They are calling you to go and show them the pictures.' So they were calling him that he should go to the government house to show them the pictures.

Because he had a camera, this was before we had television. Then he went, but after... when he came to the bus stop, he said, 'I cannot give it to you; it is very dangerous. But I promise that I will come to the house on Saturday.'

'Are you sure?'

He said, 'I'm sure.'

So there was nothing I could do; I had to leave. So I came back to my house. This was now on Thursday, and my husband said, 'I was worried. What had happened?'

I said, 'Well, the fellow refused, so I couldn't come back...even today I have come back empty-handed. But he has promised that by Saturday he will be here.'

'Oh, fine.'

We waited Friday, Saturday, he didn't come. Sunday, early in the morning, he came. He said, 'Can you come with me?'

I said, 'Fine.'

He had a car.

I went with him. We went to what used to be our office, and then behind...on each side, there was an anthill, where it was sort of bushy, we went and entered there, in the bush.

Then he pulled out that letter, a note. He said, 'This is the note.' He had written, 'I have been persuaded to be a witness of the Government. I've been forced, but as I write what I've written, whatever I have told them is not true, but I have been forced.'

Then I took that note. He said, 'As it is now, I'm leaving.'

He left immediately. I also left, went back to my house. I showed it to my husband.

'Now, what do we do?'

'Let us go and have it typed.'

We went and looked for somebody whom we knew, he typed it nicely. So we took the typed one and the original one together. We went back to our house, then my husband had to walk with it in his socks...in case we were searched.

Then we discussed the issue, said, 'We give it to one of our friends.' There was a missionary friend, Albert McAdam.' Our plan was that he should take it to the *Guardian*, because at that time, all the reporters were in Malawi. McAdam had his friend, who was a reporter and who was also sympathetic to the politicians of Nyasa at that time. He was a *Guardian* news reporter.

So we said, 'Please, if you can take this, and give it to him. Let him hide it properly.'

I left it with my husband, 'You give it to him.'

And then we had two typed ones, so we kept a typed letter, but the original and the other typed one, we gave to this man, so that he could pass it to the news reporter.

And then we said, if the reporter carried it, he would either publish it and also show it to one of the leaders of the Labour Party in Britain, in the House of Commons, because the Labour Party at that time, they were sympathetic to us. So we said, 'Let this be.'

Then that very Sunday, I said, 'My husband, now I think my duty is performed. Now I'm going.'

Two o'clock, I left for Malamulo Hospital. On Sunday. I could see that...my time now was due. I said, 'No, I cannot go to this hospital here.' (*Laughs.*) 'If I go to Queen's,[14] I don't know what will happen.'

I thought I was hiding. So I went and got a bus, went to Makwasa...to Malamulo Hospital. That Sunday, after I had done all my work, now it is final, I should go. I went to Malamulo hospital, they received me. Then on Monday...in fact at night, I slept, but not very well.

Monday morning, my baby was born. That was Monday. Tuesday—

You had gone alone to the hospital?

I went alone. I went alone. Tuesday, my husband came to see me, and he came with a journalist. It was this very same journalist from the *Guardian*. So he came, took a snap of

---

[14] By Queen's, Chibambo is referring to Queen Elizabeth Central Hospital in Blantyre. Since she was a Blantyre resident, this would have been the most obvious choice for her instead of travelling out of the city to Makwasa in Thyolo. However, she wanted to avoid government scrutiny in Blantyre.

me on the maternity bed. Then he asked me, 'In case they arrest you, what will you do?' I said, 'There's nothing. They can come and arrest me. I don't mind.'

He said, 'Are you not afraid?' I said, 'No. Everybody else is gone, so why should I be afraid? I'm only worried for my children.'

He looked at me. My husband had brought some belongings for the baby and so on. So off they went, back to Blantyre.

I don't think my husband entered the house. That was Tuesday. The morning of Wednesday, I had a certain feeling. I said, 'I don't think all is well at home.'

So then I got up; I asked the nurses if I could use their phone. So I phoned my friend, Jenny McAdam, the missionary's wife. I said, 'Do you know if Edwin is at home?' But each time I phoned she would say, 'Hallo? Halloo?' then as I explained to her, the phone cuts off. Each time I phone, I try to explain to her, the phone cuts off.

I said, 'I don't think all is well.' Then I left. I stopped. I moved back to my bed.

I saw this man and a woman. They looked at me and said, 'Ah, do you want to go home?' I looked at them.

'Oh we can help you, you know. We can help you. Can I...' the wife says, 'Can I help you to carry the baby?'

I said, 'No. Don't carry my baby. It will carry her myself.'

'Oh, can we help you to carry your *katundu*?'

Then, now I folded up the things for the baby that had come, put them in a bag, and so I said to myself...and I knew, 'Yes, I'm being arrested now. From my maternity bed.'

So then, there and then, they said, 'Let's go. We are going to take you home.'

So I just rolled up my bed and I held my baby, and they took my *katundu*. Then I was following them. The husband was in front, the wife was behind, I was in-between.

They say, 'We have a car here.' So then I went into the car. Now a poor young man, comes over to the car. He was working at Malamulo Hospital as a medical man, Mr McDonald Ngwira.[15]

He comes in, says, 'Can I have a lift to Blantyre too?'

---

[15] Rose Chibambo explained that Mr McDonald Ngwira had died a week before my interview with her.

He thought these people were just giving me a lift!

So they said, 'Alright, you can get in.'

But I knew, I said to myself, 'This is my arrest.'

As we drove from the hospital yard, went into the road, looking behind, there were so many soldiers in Jeeps. Soldiers in Jeeps with their guns high up. In front, soldiers in Jeeps, with the guns up. And our car was just in the middle, couldn't be seen. Then we drove. I had some…I had a basin where I had carried some fruits for the children.

Then…so I said, 'These are the fruits for my children.' We arrived in Limbe, near the police. So I said, 'Alright, take these fruits. Give them to a Mr Soko; he's one of the policemen in there. Say Mr Soko should take them home…to my house. If they mention my name, he will know.'

They took the basin there, quickly they came in, and we drove off.

And Mr Ngwira?

Mr Ngwira had dropped off in Limbe. And he was wondering, he thought I was also coming out. (*Laughs.*) He was just surprised, just standing. Off we went. And driving, you could not see anything, it was just racing like anything. And the soldiers were all there.

We drove right up to Zomba prison without stopping. We stopped at Zomba Prison gate. They say, 'You get out now.'

So, just coming from the maternity ward, I was wet all over. Just dripping. I tried to stand up, felt ashamed.

They said, 'Hey, come on. Get out!'

So, I came out. I staggered, came out, but still held my baby.

Came out, then they opened the door. 'Come on. Come on.'

Well, they first of all took me into a room, and they called a lady to come and inspect me. So when she came in to inspect me, she saw how I was, and, being a woman too, she was worried. This was a white woman, no black was anywhere near.

Then the captain came. So this woman said, 'You know, she must go to the hospital immediately, otherwise it's going to be a disaster. She's not well, she's bleeding so much. She must go to the hospital.'

Then the captain said, 'We cannot send her to the hospital because she's the most wanted person.'

And I was just looking at them.

They said, 'Come on, let's go.'

Then she said, 'You better call the doctor to come and examine her.'

So when the doctor came, I was still there, the captain had gone out. This woman jumped in, said to the doctor, 'Please recommend that this woman should go to the hospital.'

And the captain had to come in. Then she stood, looking elsewhere. (*Sighs.*) So the doctor examined me and he was a man. So he said, 'Ah, I think she must go to the hospital with the baby as well.'

So they just looked at him. Off the doctor went, everybody else, they went, then they pushed me, they said, 'Ah, you better go.' So they led me to a place like outside there, at the veranda, it's where we were living. Sleeping, literally a place like this (*gestures outside to her veranda*). This has even got some bricks *mphepete* but it was just an open veranda. It's where we lived for six months. *Mphepo* and everything was blowing, the baby crying all night. I lived there for two weeks before being taken to hospital. Those were the prison orders. After those two weeks, I was brought back to the veranda. Maybe it was part of the punishment.

Only one nurse was allowed to come to the hospital and that was Cecilia Kadzamira. She used to bring a jug of milk for the baby. The prison orderlies would scold her, but she took them on, told them the child needed milk. For the two weeks that I was there, she really attended to me very well.

The International Red Cross also came to check on us while we were in prison, and we were also visited by members of the British Commission of Enquiry into the massacre plot.

Our lawyer was Mr Dingle Foot who interviewed me in connection with the arrest.

I remember that on the day I was to appear before the Commission, I had a toothache. When I explained to the prison authorities, they told me, 'This is the only day assigned for them to see you.'

I went and had to face six judges, headed by Patrick Devlin.

'Why were you the only woman at the bush meeting?'

'I was representing my body, the Women's League.'

'Why was the meeting held in the bush?'

'They refused to give us a hall.'

And the final questions from Patrick Devlin: 'Do you know what you are accused of? You are accused of subversive acts. Do you understand that?'

'Yes.'

'Are you afraid?'

'No. We never plotted to kill anybody.'

Now there was a camp organised outside the prison. It was a detention camp. Two of my friends, Mrs Mdeza and Mrs Ntenda (née Nyakanyasu) were in that camp. I refused to sleep alone; I wanted to be with my friends. After days spent sleeping on the veranda, I was allowed by the authorities to join the other women in the camp, 'Sleep here. You can receive your friends, but you will have to cook your own food. You are not prisoners, but detainees.'

Vera Chirwa and Gertrude Rubadiri had also been arrested. Gertrude was pregnant at the time. I had been to school with Vera when we were at Ekwendeni. Vera was actually transferred from Harare prison to Zomba, where she stayed for two weeks before her release.

Being in prison...my baby needed food, and that was difficult to get.

You know, I will never forget the kindness of Mrs Kayes, who was a missionary's wife. I remember I asked her for powdered milk. She brought it together with towels and a basin where the baby could bath. She also brought a bottle for the baby.

Every day, Mrs Kayes would bring something for the baby. She said, 'One day I will be in prison too, and I would like someone to visit me.'

And Catherine Smith, she would say, '*Mwanayu si prisoner. Tingamtenge akapitidwe mphepo*' ('This child is not a prisoner. Let's take her so that she can get some fresh air.'). There was also Reverend Doig and his wife who went to see the men in prison.

Then there was Andrew Ross and his wife. They lent me a pram for the baby. Jenny and Albert McAdam brought me some clothes for the baby; some material and a sun suit for Gadi.

Left: Portrait of Rose Chibambo, 1963 (courtesy of Rose L Chibambo Trust)
Right: Rose and husband Edwin Chibambo, 1964 (courtesy of Rose L Chibambo Trust)

Left: Dr Hastings Kamuzu Banda returns to Nyasaland, 1958 (Malawi National Records & Archives Services)

Above: Banda (standing, right) as leader of the Nyasaland African Congress campaigning for the end of the Federation, 1958/59. Lali Lubani (far left, seated), Orton C Chirwa (center left seated), M Kanyama Chiume (centre right, white suit), Aleke K Banda (far right, partially hidden)

THE 50 MALAWI PARTY ELECTION CANDIDATES,15TH MARCH 1964

Above: Self-government legislative assembly, ca. 1961. Chibambo, first row, fourth from right (Malawi National Records & Archives Services)

Below: Malawi Party Election Candidates, 15 March 1964. Chibambo, first row, third from right (Malawi National Records & Archives Services)

Above: The aftermath of the Cabinet Crisis. Here, primary school students showing their support for Banda by vilifying Ministers who opposed Banda, possibly late 1964. The DOF, one of Banda's many titles, was Defeater of Federation. (Malawi National Records & Archives Services)

Below: Led by a Ngoni praise singer, Banda after being made Life President of Malawi, 1971 (Malawi National Records & Archives Services)

No relative was allowed to visit us. Later on, we had missionaries coming to visit us.

In prison, as I have said before, I made friends with Mrs Mdeza. She was very nice, very encouraging.

There was also a friend of ours from Karonga, Tijepani Gondwe. I had been coaching her to start a women's branch in Karonga.

If there is a painful prison, it is to be detained. We were not doing anything...just sitting. It was the most awkward thing; it is better to be working, even if for no pay. I also remember the mosquitoes; my baby had sores all over.

Everyone else was released. Later, I, too, was released, then sent to Kanjedza. My husband, who was at Kanjedza, just came to see us and then he was called to be locked up.

I was later flown to Mzuzu and then driven to Ekwendeni.

My mother had come with the children, she was there, along with mother-in-law.

Oh, the reunion with my children. They couldn't believe that they were seeing mummy. That was what the State of Emergency did to us.

I had gone through this, but there were other members of the family who had also suffered detention. My husband, at Kanjedza Detention Camp. My brother-in-law, BaQabaniso, at Port Herald. Each holiday, during Christmas, we had to go to Port Herald to try and cheer him up.

BaQabaniso used to say, 'No prisoner can be freed if he's good. A political prisoner can only be freed with politics.'

What drove you to go on in spite of the problems you faced?

I really took it to be my duty to perform. I had this feeling that there is need for women to understand... It is indeed something that one cannot understand. Even today I still see that women do not have courage. What stops them, I don't know.

God has given us a life and a duty to perform... If I feel it myself, I can't say, '*Iwe*, can you do that...' I saw that our people were suffering.

The problem was not the missionaries; we accepted them as part of us. But it was the colour bar, which I experienced when I came to the South. You know, seeing people shopping from a window, people being pushed from the land they had lived on, especially in Thyolo.

And then thangata, children would be doing thangata.

All the fertile land would be taken by the settlers. I could see that a lot of problems were coming for the African people. A small white child would be calling to a grown up person, 'You, boy!' There would be notices, 'Palibe njira,' so that a black person should not pass.

Our aim was therefore to fight against the Federation and to gain independence.

Now, something I need to say about the party. While we were in prison, Shadreck Khonje and Augustine Mthambala kept the party going secretly because it was banned. Ceciwa Bwanausi [Khonje] worked very hard to keep the fire burning. Those people outside were very sympathetic to us all. When Vera Chirwa and her husband, Orton Ching'oli, were released, they were approached by Ceciwa Bwanausi, Shadreck Khonje and Augustine Mthambala who asked them to take over, which they did.

That's when the party became Malawi Congress Party. Vera had to organise the Women's League. She took on the women's wing and kept moving. Vera therefore joined the Women's League after her release. Orton Ching'oli Chirwa was not the first president of the MCP, but he and Vera brought the party out into the open upon request from Mthambala, Khonje and Bwanausi.

Vera revamped the Women's League. She had quite a strong executive, Mrs Violet Chavura and Mrs Hudson, a very nice girl, active.

Violet Chavura was a very active and intelligent person. This group carried the party until we came out. Later in the year, after many of us had been released, Kamuzu Banda held a conference in Nkhotakota. It was there, when we were receiving the last of the detainees, that it was then announced that the former prisoners would take over their positions.

About that last group of detainees: Chipembere and the Chisiza brothers. Did you know that they would be released and that they would join you during the conference in September 1960?

No, we didn't know. I think only Kamuzu Banda knew, and he wanted to surprise us at the conference. It was indeed a surprise; they were indeed the prison graduates, as they were called.

Perspectives on the Meeting in the Bush and the Subsequent Arrests

There are many accounts about what was really discussed during the meeting in the bush. For example, the Federal Government referred to the meeting as the 'murder plot,' stating that members of the Nyasaland African Congress had actually planned to kill whites, Asians and moderate Africans in the event of Kamuzu Banda's arrest. Those who held this view included secretary of state, Alan Lennox-Boyd, who spoke in the House of Commons justifying the State of Emergency which was declared in Nyasaland on 3 March 1959.[i] Those who subscribed to this view mostly based it on intelligence reports made by the Special Branch in Nyasaland.

Another school of thought was that the Federal Government wanted to suppress dissent of any type, and thus, through Welensky, pressurised Governor Armitage into declaring a State of Emergency. Among those who held this view were members of the opposition Labour Party in Britain.[ii]

One cannot discuss the meeting in the bush or the State of Emergency without referring to the Devlin Report of 22 July 1959. The Devlin Commission was led by a High Court judge, Lord Patrick Arthur Devlin, with the purpose of investigating the reasons behind the State of Emergency. Murphy notes that the Devlin Report was sceptical about the idea of a murder plot and cast 'significant doubt' on the way in which the colonial government gathered information about the meeting.[iii] The report called into question the presence of some informants at the meeting, while others, such as Kalua, the man Chibambo referred to, were unreliable informants. Chibambo touches on this unreliability when she recounts how, several times, he failed to keep his promise to write a letter recanting the information he had given to the police. Despite this, the police believed that Kalua had told the truth but had been intimidated into recanting by Chibambot.[iv] Nonetheless, as Colin Baker has argued, the Commission exonerated the colonial government for declaring a State of Emergency, although this may not have been immediately apparent in the scathing sections of the report.[v] The Commission also noted that one of the resolutions at the meeting had been to resist the actions of the government with violence. This reference to violence has also been included in a study by Simpson,[vi] as well as by Kayira and Chiudza.[vii]

Over 50 Africans were killed during the State of Emergency, and 1,322 people were arrested. Amongst those who were arrested were key members of the Nyasaland African Congress, including Banda and Chibambo.

If the meeting in the bush shows differing perspectives in terms of cause, the same can be said about reports of the arrests. The following are two accounts of Rose Chibambo's arrest:

> Another of the Four
>
> Mrs Rose Chibambo, one of the four Congress officials named by the

governor, Sir Robert Armitage, to launch 'R' Day was detained under the Emergency Regulations Act last Sunday after being discharged from Malamulo Mission hospital.

Last week she gave birth there to a baby girl. Mrs Chibambo was removed to Zomba central prison where there are facilities for her. Mrs Chibambo was leader of the Women's League.[viii]

The idea of 'another' in the headline suggests continuity with earlier arrests; Masauko Chipembere, Dunduzu Chisiza and Kanyama Chiume had already been arrested. Chibambo's arrest was covered in a different manner by *Jet* magazine:

> British seize African mother after childbirth
>
> In Salisbury, Southern Rhodesia, British security forces arrested the top woman in the outlawed Nyasaland Africa National Congress as she walked out of a hospital after giving birth to her fifth child. She was 29 year old Mrs Rose Chibambo, Chairman of the Women's section of the Nyasaland Congress, which was banned a month ago when a State of Emergency was declared in the British protectorate to crush a nationalist uprising. Her husband, Samuel, was seized a week ago.[ix]

Some of the facts in *Jet* were inaccurate, such as the reference to Southern Rhodesia instead of Malamulo in Thyolo, Nyasaland, and the reference to Samuel instead of Edwin. Nonetheless, the tone of these news excerpts reflects the views of the owners; *Jet* was notable for chronicling the American Civil Rights movement, whereas the *Nyasaland Times* tended to be pro-government.

The arrest was also memorialised through song, although this happened after Chibambo's release. Zondiwe Mbano recalls a song that schoolchildren sung prior to independence:

> *NyaZiba wakakana*
>
> *Na mpakana ku gadi*
>
> *Kamuzu wakakana*
>
> *Na mpakana ku gadi.*
>
> (NyaZiba refused [Federation]
>
> All the way to jail
>
> Kamuzu refused [Federation]
>
> All the way to jail.)[x]

TIME IN PRISON

Chapter 13

The Role of Music and Dance in Politics

LOMATHINDA

ROLE OF MUSIC AND DANCE

*T*here has often been a lot of debate on whether women should dance through political rallies. What was the position of the Women's League on dancing at political gatherings prior to independence?

Dancing is part of the African people when they are socialising. Even if you look at the Ngoni hymns, you will see that they were often accompanied by dance. Now things have been exaggerated.

During our time, we used to sing to show that we were supporting Kamuzu. Unfortunately it went to his head. We gave him a lot of praise in order to show the Europeans that we could support our leader.

I would stand up and say, 'Kamuzu wawina, wawina. Welensike manyazi.' ('Kamuzu has won. Shame on Welensky.') We were building him.

We used to feel that the whites did not respect each other and could not rule each other.

I had a chance to see some of the letters that politicians were writing to Kamuzu at the time and noted the tone of reverence that was used. There were those who called him 'Father.' For instance, one sees that term in Masauko Chipembere's letters. Was that the case in the party, that you all treated Kamuzu with reverence?

Each one of us was writing him as an individual; perhaps that is how Chipembere knew him. Chipembere must have been writing that when he was in prison.

You know, there was a time, just after independence, when Chipembere was talking during a meeting. The Queen was in the country, and during that function, Chipembere started to make a rather fiery speech. I saw Kamuzu trying to touch Chip's foot as a way of saying, 'Don't say that.'

I respected Kamuzu, but there were certain things I didn't do. For example, I never knelt to him. It doesn't mean that I didn't respect him.

What do you remember about those early days when it became clear that the Malawi Congress Party would rule the country?

I remember that before independence, when Kamuzu was Prime Minister, Dunduzu Chisiza was Parliamentary Secretary to the Minister of Finance. When you were Parliamentary Secretary, you were understudying the Minister of that particular section.

I remember that Dunduzu organised a symposium where key economists came to

Malawi. It was quite a successful symposium. Unfortunately he died soon after that symposium, in a car accident.

Details of that accident...it was really difficult to come to terms with. There are some things that you always remember, for me it was the fact that this was someone we had started out with together. I also remember that he had come to visit me a day or two before the accident, but my husband and I had been out. And then the next thing, you hear he's dead. Unbelievable. He was such an intelligent man. I remember he once told me that although we were really excited about independence, we might be disillusioned afterwards. And you know the strange thing? He was saying, 'You' meaning those in our group. He wasn't saying, 'We,' wasn't including himself in the group. I remember that.

Most of us were MPs as the time for independence drew near. I was MP for Mzimba Central. I was later assigned to the Ministry of Natural Resources and Community Development, which was headed by Kamuzu. The Ministry of Natural Resources was responsible for social welfare, community development, hospitals and prisons. I was Parliamentary Secretary. You could say that a Parliamentary Secretary was the equivalent of a deputy minister.

I also remember that as members of the Women's League, we used to go to Blantyre Market, just to sweep the premises. We wanted a clean environment, so we would do this regularly.

Were you ever Official Hostess?[16]

No. I was never an official hostess. Before the State of Emergency, the Official Hostess was Elizabeth Mwase.

A person comes in the way Banda came to Malawi. You all say, 'hohoho!' Then everybody scatters and goes home. Who is left to look after him? It all fell in the hands of Yatuta Chisiza, the party's Administrative Secretary. He took care of Banda. Not many people were willing to go to prison. They were afraid.

People talk because they don't know what used to happen. People carried the party as if it was their own baby.

---

[16] The term 'Official Hostess' was used for the female administrator whose duties included overseeing Kamuzu Banda's household, being present at official functions, welcoming guests and accompanying him during his travels. As Chibambo has pointed out, Cecilia Kadzamira, later to be known as Mama, became Official Hostess after Mwase. Kadzamira continued as Official Hostess after independence, and the title became Government Official Hostess (GOH). Her duties were extended to include chairing *Chitukuko Cha Amayi M'Malawi*, an organisation founded by Banda with the aim of empowering women. She remained with Banda until his death in 1997.

Kamuzu had nobody. A home was found for him; he sat there. The person who took care of Banda's welfare was Yatuta. Yet, later on, Yatuta died, shot by soldiers in the newly independent Malawi, in the same country that Banda was now ruling...

To go back to those early days, Elizabeth Mwase was found much later to take care of Kamuzu's household, to talk to the servants.

Elizabeth left after the State of Emergency; she was engaged and wanted to get married. After Emergency, Yatuta brought in Cecilia Kadzamira. Cecilia had to be found; she was a good person who took care of people. She was brought to Dr Banda. Cecilia didn't come to look for a job, she was persuaded.

John Tembo was not known at the time, didn't join us.

Don't think of what is happening today...we had to fight for you to have the universities, and then someone is insulting us to say, 'Sanaphunzire awa.' ('These people are not educated.')

And then the other thing that I also wanted clarification on, and this is related to the newspapers. I saw that, especially come 1965, the Women's League was often referred to as the 'Amazon Army'. Was that there when you were chairperson of the group?

The Amazon Army, yes. It was there. Each time Dr Banda was addressing a meeting, he would point at me, 'This is my Amazon Army.' We had this name. The League was known as the Amazon Army.

So it was a name you accepted.

We accepted it. We didn't know it; we accepted it just as it was. (*Laughs.*) He said, 'They are biting.' It was part of encouragement, you know. He said, 'These women are the Amazon Army; they bite. Then Welensky cannot get anywhere near.' This was more during the time when the political crisis was at its climax.

It was part of...what would I say...part of Dr Banda praising us. Praising our activity.

During that time, things were well. It's very unfortunate; I don't know what came to his mind, but he started well.

Anticipating Independence

The early 1960s were a time of change for the Nyasaland nationalists in many ways. Most of them, including Chibambo, had spent the beginning of 1959 in prison and were released at the end of the year or in 1960. Banda, for instance, was released in April 1960.

Change, as referred to above, included the party itself. The Nyasaland African Congress had been banned during the State of Emergency and was revived under a new name: the Malawi Congress Party. It was chaired by Orton Chirwa during the time when Banda was in prison. Chirwa later handed over the party to Banda soon after the latter's release. Orton Chirwa's wife, Vera, chaired the Women's League of the Malawi Congress Party, and during her time, the League expanded to include 11 branches. Although Chibambo had been released at this time, she was based in Mzimba. In October 1960, however, Chibambo took over as chair of the League on Banda's insistence.[i] She also became the only female member of the Malawi Congress Party's National Executive.

McCracken writes that one of the noticeable changes in the party included income generation; the party had 22 Land Rovers, a press company and a newspaper.[ii] The Malawi Congress Party also had money from entrance and annual subscription fees as well as the sale of Kamuzu badges.[iii]

Banda now had a power base, and his party was able to campaign for positions in the Legislative Council. In 1960, he was declared Life President of the Malawi Congress Party. In August 1961, the Malawi Congress Party became the ruling party after winning five seats when it competed against the United Christian Federation and the Christian Democratic Party. At this stage, the country was not yet independent, but the Congress' triumph meant that the country could secede from the Federation. It also meant that while the country was still under colonial rule, Banda, who was not yet Prime Minister, was effectively in charge and could choose ministerial positions. Banda gave himself two ministerial portfolios: Minister of Natural Resources and Minister of Local Government. Other ministerial appointments made in 1961 included that of Kanyama Chiume as Education Minister, Mikeka Mkandawire as Minister without portfolio, Augustine Bwanausi as Minister of Labour, Dunduzu Chisiza as Parliamentary Secretary of Finance and Colin Cameron, a Scottish lawyer, as Minister of Works. In retrospect, Cameron had this to say about those early days,

> ...One thing in all the queries that arise about that time is the emphasis on the independence Cabinet. This is important, but Kamuzu had been effectively in charge for the three years leading up to Independence, and it was at that time the preparation and ground work was done.

With the Cabinet Crisis arriving so soon after Independence, it deflected from the day to day running of their ministries. A truer reflection on their abilities can be gleaned from the pre-independence years 1961 to 1964. The months from July to Nov 1964 were all a political turmoil.

The reason I say this is that from the outset Kamuzu in 1961, because of the outcome of the first elections, could never be outvoted in the Cabinet, and the Governor had to respect that.'[iv]

On the eve of Independence, Kamuzu Banda, by then Prime Minister, made a speech during a state luncheon, talking about what the country had been through under colonialism. The speech focused mostly on his struggles, but he also made reference to Rose Chibambo: 'You see that woman over there—Rose Chibambo—she organised her Women's League. There is Chindongo—he organised my youth.'[v]

Below is a line-up of Banda's cabinet in 1963, the year before independence:

Prime Minister: Dr H Kamuzu Banda

Minister of Trade and Industry: Dr H Kamuzu Banda

Minister of Natural Resources, Surveys and Social Development: Dr H Kamuzu Banda

Minister of Home Affairs: Yatuta Chisiza

Minister of Housing and Development: Augustine Bwanausi

Minister of Transport and Communications: John Msonthi

Minister of Works: Colin Cameron

Minister of External Affairs: Kanyama Chiume

Minister of Education: Masauko Chipembere

Minister of Labour: Willie Chokani

Minister of Finance: John Tembo

Parliamentary Secretary for Natural Resources, Surveys and Social Development: Rose Chibambo.[vi]

Dunduzu Chisiza died two years before Malawi's independence. He was someone who had pondered what would happen to Africa after independence. Below is an extract from his pamphlet, published in 1962, from which he gave his presentation at the symposium barely two months before his death:

> ...only a high degree of moral integrity and a sense of proportion among the leaders can ensure that they will not turn themselves into dictators. The temptation to assume dictatorial powers in new countries is great. It may come about because citizens are not trusting enough or because they are too trusting. It may be backed by good or ghastly motives. Whatever the cause and whatever the motive behind the temptation, only honesty of purpose, moral integrity, selflessness, humility, patience and solicitude can nip malice in the bud, annihilate the power mania...[vii]

ROLE OF MUSIC AND DANCE

Chapter 14

The Cabinet Crisis
1964

THE CABINET CRISIS

It was the saddest thing. Malawi got independent first, before Zambia and Mozambique. But then what happened soon after independence was really sad.

There were some problems in our country. Mozambicans, South Africans and Zimbabweans wanted to hide in Malawi during their fight against the colonial regimes in their countries. Kamuzu didn't want this. Party members would say, 'Let's welcome our friends, give them space to stay.' Kamuzu didn't want that. That used to eat me up. Kwame Nkrumah had assisted us. Banda forgot this.

Another problem concerned African government officials who had worked with the Europeans. Some Europeans had understudied from Africans. There came a time for our people to feel independent; some of the people needed to be given a department. Dr Banda refused to let black people take over a department. And we used to say, 'How will people know that we're independent when they are doing all the work and the white man is just sitting?'

At that time, the permanent secretaries were still white men, so whatever you said, he would still want to hear from the permanent secretaries. He trusted the permanent secretaries more that he trusted his own ministers.

So that was also something that, having discovered, most of the men—I should say, the ministers—were not happy about. Because they would be reporting to their president, now why should the president trust the permanent secretary more than me, a minister? Because I would tell him things as I see them? Now a white man might see things from a different perspective.

That was the time that people were hearing that he said, '*Mutu biii*! No, not an African to run a department. No! *Mutu bii*! No.'

So these were part of the things and when you tried...whenever they tried to say, 'Alright, these are the things; let us go and present them together,' then that was an issue with Dr Banda. He didn't like to be corrected.

He refused it, and that was part of the problem. So he thought, since the ministers had suggested it, and he was against it, then he felt that it means they are now organising against him with the people, to rise against him. That was the whole issue.

Here's something I need clarification on: I read that before the cabinet crisis, some members of the cabinet had already approached Banda about some of the problems that were there. As a result of that meeting, he offered to resign as prime minister, but the ministers apparently told him that there was no need for resignation. But soon afterwards the cabinet members met at Ku Chawe in order to come up with more demands. Were you part of the team that met at Ku Chawe?

No. I didn't attend that meeting. The main thing is that...we would say...we would complain...or we would question. It was now this time as we were coming up. I would say he had started doubting us.

He was now getting closer to the whites. Although part of the things, you know, he was being fed by some of our people. This too, he invited it himself. It is always dangerous if you want people to be telling you lies or to say, 'Whatever so-and-so is saying, please come and let me know.' Then they will come and tell you even lies.

I know there was a time that he was always fond of saying, 'Well, my boys, my boys...' even in Parliament he would say, 'Oh well, my boys...' This was when he was referring to my friends, the ministers.

So they didn't like it. They felt that perhaps he just kept on belittling them as if they were not intelligent enough to think for themselves. Because each time you tried to talk to Dr Banda about things that are happening in your department, he would not trust you.

But then you've talked about these men, and the way in which he was resentful over their presentation of issues, and how he didn't like to be corrected. But what about you? Is there anything you ever tried to correct him on?

No. Uhm, not on my own, but as a group. But still, he felt...he felt as if I was somehow a threat. I remember there was a time when he introduced a tickey[17] (threepence)... when he introduced that tickey in Parliament. It was during the time when we were discussing the Ministry of Health.

Kamuzu wanted to introduce a system whereby people would pay a tickey in hospitals. We discussed it, then we left.

But I was concerned and went back to him. I suggested that since this had been introduced, it would affect women more because of the children and even themselves; they were the ones who would be going to the hospital. So I suggested that I should to go and sensitise the women, that this is what they would be expected to do. I wanted to tell them that they should not get upset or wonder, but that the tickey was the only way

---

[17] The tickey was the equivalent of the threepence fee that Dr Banda suggested be paid by people in Malawi in order to access hospital services. Weeks after being introduced in 1964, it caused a lot of resentment because, before independence, people had not been required to pay anything at public hospitals. The justification behind the fee was that the new government did not have enough money to subsidise hospital services (Richard Tambulasi, 'Policy Transfer, Path Dependence and veto Points: The Politics of Hospital Autonomy Reforms in Malawi,' Paper presented at Public Administrative Committee Conference on Competing Narratives of Public Service Reform, University of Glamorgan, 7–9 September, 2009, pp. 23–24). Banda had been acting upon recommendation from the Skinner Report (mentioned in this chapter), but withdrew the fee upon realising how unpopular it was.

we could try to help in the development of our country.

He agreed with me, 'Oh, yes, I think you're right. You'd better go indeed.'

I left for Karonga, together with some of my friends in the Executive. While we were in Karonga, we called a meeting, addressed the women. Then we retired, in the hope that that evening, we would now be moving to Rumphi. It was during that evening that the MPs of Karonga came to me. Mr Adamson Kanyanya, one of the MPs, told me, 'Parliament is meeting. Parliament is meeting tomorrow.'

I said, 'What?'

'Yes. Parliament is meeting. It's an emergency.'

'Why? We have just closed Parliament. Now why is it so?'

'Well, we are just telling you that this is the issue.'

Then we had to start off, and we moved the whole night, reached Blantyre in the morning.

Now that morning, I was now getting ready to go to Parliament. (*Sighs.*) Before I went, the Speaker of the House, Aleck Nyasulu, came to my house. He told me that it was very good that I had come. And he said, 'You better go and meet the president. You were not here.'

I said, 'What's wrong? Cos I'm told Parliament is meeting.'

He said, 'Yes. Parliament is meeting, but first of all, you better go and see the president, and tell him the news about the North, that the whole country is behind him. Because the ministers have actually annoyed him. They have told him that the country is not happy because of this tickey.'

Banda used to bring things to the Parliament before they were discussed in cabinet. I said, 'You mean the ministers have annoyed him? Therefore he wants me to go and reassure him?'

He says, 'Yes.'

I said, 'No, I'm not going to see him unless I meet my friends first and hear what they said to him that has annoyed him. But that I should just stand up and go to him and say, 'Ah, no, all is well in the North with you', to me it makes no sense. I must know first what has happened. I have worked with my friends, I know that they are obedient to Kamuzu.'

That was enough. So when the Speaker of the House went and told him that I had refused, then he knew that they had cooked these things together.

'They' meaning you and the other cabinet members.

Meaning me and my colleagues. Banda said, 'It means they ganged together against me. Why does she not come? Because these others came when she was away. So I wanted to hear what she was going to say.'

I said, 'No, I just can't go and say, "All is well with you." No.' (*Laughs*.)

So my aim was that I should first of all meet my friends, and then we would discuss and say, 'We had this meeting, and this is what transpired.' But before that, how do I do it?

So, then we left. We all went to Parliament. And while we were there, then they said, 'Ah, no, Parliament is not meeting today. Not until tomorrow.'

So we were just there. Then we said, 'Ah ah. What has happened? Then why call us?'

That day, we went back home. As I went back home from Zomba, getting to Blantyre, I got there, found my daughter, Malibase. Now, she was crying. Others were just saying, 'Aha, this one too.'

I said, 'Why are you crying?'

She said, 'Mummy, you've been dismissed.'

I said, 'Dismissed? What?'

She said, 'Yes, they are saying on the radio that you have been dismissed by Dr Banda. What has happened?'

I said, 'That is news. I've not been told.'

So indeed, when the seven o'clock news came, there it was: 'Ching'oli Chirwa, Kanyama Chiume, Augustine Bwanausi and Rose Chibambo have been dismissed from the MCP and as members of parliament.'

So the next morning, when we all went, we sat as backbenchers. Out of loyalty, Yatuta and Chokani sat with us.

I said, 'I have heard my dismissal from the radio. Nobody has told me.' Then while there, I was served with a notice of dismissal. (*Laughs*.) By the permanent secretary who was Peter Youens.

I think Kamuzu had already planned to dismiss us. It was a terrible moment.

The things some of the people were saying! 'You people from the North, we don't know how you will get to your region, you will have to pass through our constituencies. We shall deal with you Ghana style.' Ah! It was terrible.

Anyway it was a terrible moment and a very sad moment. That after all that we had worked for, and it should end up just in the way it did. No, we couldn't believe it.

When you said someone said they would deal with you 'Ghana style,' what had happened in Ghana? What was meant by 'Ghana style'?

I don't know. This was Yakobo's wife,[18] 'Oh, Ghana style.' Together with Yakobo. Anyway, today I just take them that they were the victims of circumstances.

About Ghana, they were referring to Nkrumah's time, when he was...I think, when there was a coup and they took over from him. But I don't know exactly what it meant. But it was really surprising; people had already been organised to take over from us. We couldn't believe it.

That man...hmm.

In my view, Kamuzu was a very scared man and he was afraid that we were going to overthrow him. I'm talking here about people like Chokani, Bwanausi and Ching'oli. I can't talk about Aleke;[19] he was quite young at the time.

But you see, the problems I was talking about, these were things we could have discussed; there was no need for a crisis.

---

[18] Yakobo is used as a pseudonym; Chibambo mentioned the name of Yakobo and his wife but did not want the names to be included in the book.
[19] Aleke Banda was a Malawian politician who served under President Kamuzu Banda and, later on, President Bakili Muluzi. He had a keen interest in journalism, founding *Malawi News*, which later became the government newspaper during Kamuzu's time, and then *The Nation* in 1993. He and Banda were shareholders of Malawi Press Limited (See McCracken, *A History of Malawi*, pp. 369–370). Among his political positions were the following: Secretary-General of the Malawi Congress Party, Finance Minister and Minister Agriculture during Bakili Muluzi's presidency. He later became president of the People's Progressive Movement (PPM) after leaving Muluzi's United Democratic Front (UDF).

Tensions in a New Nation

Rose Chibambo captured the essence of what the Cabinet Crisis was all about: delayed Africanisation, Banda's friendly relations with the Portuguese, his refusal to establish relations with China, his acceptance of the tickey, and a rather patronising attitude towards his ministers. Some of these aspects, such as the tickey, were part of the Skinner Report which had been commissioned to investigate reforms in the civil service (see below). The reference to 'my boys' as he called the ministers, is one that has also been noted in several historical records. As early as 1961, Banda had started declaring that he was 'father' to 'the boys' and had pointed out that only he could make policy.[i] He would also intervene in Parliament in order to correct the ministers' pronunciation of English.[ii]

On 10 August 1964, the ministers met with Banda and presented their complaints regarding his policies and his attitude towards them. They felt their complaints had been heard because his response was 'muted.'[iii] Three weeks later, on 26 August, the ministers, emboldened by the initial meeting, confronted Banda during a cabinet meeting. Chipembere was absent from the meeting as he was attending a conference in Canada. Chiume, Chisiza and Chirwa were the ones who spoke out, although at times John Tembo[20] also aired supporting views.[iv] As a result of the meeting, Banda offered to resign, but the ministers stated that this was not why they had raised different issues with him. A day later, the ministers, except for Tembo, met at Ku Chawe Inn in Zomba and drew up what was known as the 'Kuchawe Manifesto' on action points that they wanted Banda to address. By this time, however, Banda had started receiving support from party loyalists in Parliament, and he made a decision to dismiss the cabinet members he saw as the trouble-makers. Chibambo, who had not attended any of these meetings, was regarded as organising women's groups against him. Her trip to Karonga was viewed as a plot to get women in the North to protest against the tickey.

Below are excerpts from speeches made by Kamuzu Banda and Rose Chibambo during the parliamentary debate that was held on 8 and 9 September 1964 as a

---

[20] In 1963, John Tembo, Cecilia Tamanda Kadzamira's uncle, was the youngest member of Kamuzu Banda's cabinet. He joined the Malawi Congress Party after the 'young Turks' had already established themselves. He rose through the ranks, becoming a powerful figure in the Malawi Congress Party. He also became Kamuzu Banda's Chichewa interpreter at official functions. For a long time after Kamuzu Banda's death, he was president of the Malawi Congress Party.

result of the meetings that have been discussed above. Chibambo was the first of the dismissed parliamentarians to speak in parliament.[v]

Kamuzu Banda's Speech

The Prime Minister (Dr Banda): Mr Speaker, Sir, it is with deep grief that I rise to speak this morning. I arise to speak in sorrow and grief because the four cornerstones on which the Malawi Congress Party, the Government—yes, even more—our State, the State of Malawi itself was built, has (sic) broken down; has broken down.

What are the four cornerstones on which our Party, Our Government, Our State, was built? Here they are. Unity, loyalty, discipline and obedience. These are the four cornerstones on which destruction of the Malawi Congress Party—destruction of the Malawi Government, destruction of the Malawi State itself, Mr Speaker, stands. Once these four cornerstones are broken away, one by one, the obedience, unity, loyalty, discipline, responsibility, there is no Malawi Congress Party. There is no Government, no Malawi Government in this country, and there is no State, the State of Malawi. What do we get? Another Congo? Is that what anyone in this country wants? (*Interjection: No! No!*)

I just want everyone to know in this House and to keep in mind what makes this country different from any other country in East and Central Africa. It is these four cornerstones on which we first built the old Nyasaland African Congress Party of 1958, when I was elected Life President at Nkata, and then the succeeding Party to the old Congress, the Malawi Congress Party. I said at Rangeley Stadium that if we have got our independence, if we have defeated Welensky, if we have broken the stupid Federation, it was due to these four things—unity, loyalty, discipline and obedience. (*Hear! Hear!*) (*Loud applause.*)

I say I stand in sorrow and grief, Mr Speaker. Look at those strange faces. Among

---

[21] The Skinner Report was a series of recommendations on the civil service made by James Skinner, a high court judge. Kamuzu Banda's government implemented the report in 1964. Some of the unpopular aspects of the recommendations included introducing pegged salary scales for civil servants and a contributory pension scheme that replaced the non-contributory scheme used before 1964. The contributory scheme meant that civil servants would have a salary cut of five per cent. (See Ken Barnes, A Rough Passage, Vol. II: Memories of Empire, London, Radcliffe Press 2007, pp. 85–86).

them you see new faces—Kumtumanji over there, Chidzanja over there. Among the old Members only John Tembo and John Msonthi are with me. I would rather see those benches empty and myself in the bush, dead, than see these four cornerstones destroyed by anyone. Once there is no unity, no loyalty, no discipline, no obedience, we are finished; we are finished. Just as the Congo. It is finished. [...]

Only 26th of August, Mr Speaker, there was a Cabinet Meeting in the room which you know, in this very building. At that Cabinet Meeting there were a number of papers to be discussed—among them a paper on education. In the absence of the Minister of Education in Ottawa, I presented that paper on education, which was a draft Bill, to establish in this country a University, the University of Malawi. It was that draft Bill to create the University of Malawi that sparked off the smouldering embers of disunity, disloyalty, indiscipline, disobedience, which I have noticed on my return from Cairo. [...]

My Ministers turned it into a general discussion on my policies since we became self-governing and particularly since we became independent on July 6. They attacked me on two fronts, on the domestic scene and on the foreign scene. On the domestic scene, they attacked me on charges in the hospital, Africanization, the Skinner Report. On the external or foreign scene, they attacked my policy in relation to Southern Rhodesia, Portugal, Peking China and Formosa China. They told me that there was unrest in the country, resentment and bitterness among the people all over the country from Karonga to Port Herald, from Nkhota Kota to Mchinji because they said that I was charging tickies when people go to hospital...

On the external scene, they were even more furious with me. Why was I having any diplomatic relations with Portugal; why did I have a man in Mozambique representing us; why did I have my Airways going to Beira; why did I have talks with the Portuguese on trade? On Peking China and Formosa China, they demanded to know why I had not recognized the Peking China regime, there was only one China, they said, and that was Peking China...

I could not believe that it was my Ministers speaking to Kamuzu. I just couldn't believe it, Mr Speaker. Youens was there and the Clerk to the cabinet was there. You know, I am not always so sweet, but that morning I tried my best to be sweet, to be calm. I let them have their way. They talked, talked, talked, I butting in, answering here, answering there. [...]

Friday 4.30 or 5 Mr Chirwa came to my house. He told me part of the document was still to come, because they hadn't finished something. He gave me a copy of their

Bill of Indictment against me, because that is what it was, and began to read from his book...They accused me of running the Government as if it were my personal estate. They accused me of nepotism, favouritism, and they demanded equal and even distribution of Ministries. I must confess I was staggered. I, Kamuzu, practising nepotism, favouritism...[...]

By Friday afternoon I began to receive anonymous letters saying: "Please, Sir, please, Sir, do not listen to what your Ministers are saying. It is not true that there is unrest, resentment and bitterness against the Government because of the tickey. It is not true that there is unrest among Civil Servants because you are not Africanizing... What is true is that your Ministers are inciting the people deliberately...(*Hear! Hear!*) (*Applause.*) (*Interjection: That is true, Sir!*)...your own Ministers, Kanyama Chiume, Ching'oli Chirwa, Yatuta Chisiza, Augustine Bwanausi, Rose Chibambo and other people..."...so what do they do? They organize my women wrongly. Rose Chibambo is commissioned to organise my own women against me, but I am glad, very glad that the majority of my women are not fools...They do not agree with her. (*Applause.*)

The only people to whom I will surrender my power is to you. (*Applause.*) When you say you don't want me here I will go, but I will not surrender my powers to Kanyama Chiume ...(*Loud cheers*)...or Yatuta Chisiza or Augustine Bwanausi or Rose Chibambo...(*Loud cheers*)...

I have said that I am a marked man; that we are a marked people. Well, I am not afraid, I am not afraid at all. I am not afraid because I am protected by you—my people. (*Prolonged applause.*) (*Singing.*)

Rose Chibambo's Speech

Mrs Rose Chibambo (Mzimba Central): Mr Speaker, Sir, I am rising here as a back-bencher...(*Interjection: Yes, you are!*)...to speak on the motion that has been moved by the Prime Minister, and the only statement—the only words that I have heard today. I have come back to be a back-bencher today, after hearing from—I should say after hearing what has been said. I got it just as a hearsay that I am no more a Member of Parliament; I am no more a Parliamentary Secretary. (*Interjections.*)

I am speaking as Mrs Chibambo, who was there before the Ngwazi came, with the same feeling that I'm standing here today.

Most of the things that have been said here are quite strange to me. (*Interjections.*)

Mr Speaker: This is our House. We do not recognize you here, and you will not shout. It is the Members alone who shout; so I just want to warn you.

Mrs Rose Chibambo: Today is the 8th September and to me it is a day when I was born and it is a day that I am exposed to such a situation in which I am. I have always, I always, in the past, have been with the Prime Minister. I gave all my services that I would want to give as an honest follower of the nation of Malawi, an honest follower of the Ngwazi Kamuzu Banda...(*Interjection.*)...which I am up to this day.

Even though some of the Members say I have failed, I have not failed, and I will never fail.

I must always speak only the truth and it is only the truth we will appreciate to say (*sic*)... I am really disgusted...(*Interjection.*)...with the statements that have been made... Because most of the people that have been mentioned I know. Most of them are those interested in this chair where I am sitting and where I have been. I was appointed as a national Chairman of the League of Malawi...(*Interjection: So what!*)... and I honestly worked until the day that this State of Emergency was declared. I gave myself to buy this thing, even for this itself because I knew what I was doing. I was not doing those services because other people were doing them but because I dedicated myself to the cause of the nation and to the leader. Who says that I am there to...(*inaudible*). I did not care about my family, neither did I care about my children, whom I left suffering while I was fighting for the good of the people. (*Interjection: You are not alone.*) No matter, I was arrested. (*Interjection: You were not arrested.*) No matter, I was taken from the maternity ward, from labour, and put into prison. I did not care because I knew what I was doing. Not for the sake of myself but for the sake of the nation and leader, we must be free and let us get what we should get.

I am very sure that I can stand here, talking about these things, being put in a situation, being regarded as a traitor which I am not and never have been. (*Interjection: You are.*) If I have been there, I am sorry that some of the women who have been included in this are those who cannot speak for themselves in this house. If I went up North, I am sorry that people have given information to the Prime Minister the wrong way. I did not go up North to organise the women against the tickey. If the truth is there, the truth must speak and must always be known. I went over there as I did normally, having elections in Rumpi, having elections in Karonga District. Of course, I passed through my constituency which people (*sic*) I am supposed to represent and I had to address them. If you want to press the truth, never did I speak against the people. It was the people, they had to give me their complaints as their representative about which I have not even spoken about with the Prime Minister that these are the complaints that people have in my constituency. When I was making elections in Rumphi, in Karonga, women had their own complaints of which I have been prepared to bring them to the P.M. that this is what they say. There was a time that I addressed the women in the Colby Community Centre in Blantyre with the Committee, including Mrs Mann, who was with me.... If they want to face the truth, did I speak about the tickey or did I mention something about the hospital? Mr Speaker, Sir, it is disgusting. Let us face truth if we want to know the truth, and if we want the truth, the truth will always speak....I am not a person who can be easily deceived or bought by anyone. (*Interjection: They have succeeded.*) If it was possible, I should have been bought during this trouble before we came to where we are. I stood to suffer. I accepted to suffer. Even my husband accepted to suffer. Many people were getting what they were getting because they accepted that they would rather have money than speak the truth. Why should I do that today when we are independent? (*Interjection: You want more power.*) [...]

I, as I am, I am standing here, speaking for a constituency where I am supposed to stand as their representative in this house and if I have been talking to women, well let those women come forward and say, "Yes, you told us something against the Ngwazi." When and where? How could I do it only today! This is very surprising to me...(*Interjection: Hard luck for you*)...I am not worried. (*Interjection.*) I have never changed my colours ever since I identified myself with the cause, for the liberation of this country. I have never. Perhaps some of the Members who are speaking here have been changing every now and then but not me. (*Interjection.*) But I came to know that there was something when Mr Nyasulu, sitting as the Speaker, came to me and said that there was something afoot, the Ministers are rising against the Ngwazi, it was 11 o'clock at night. I did not know anything. (*Interjection: what did you do?*) [...]

Mr Speaker, Sir, if we want to be honest in this country, if we want to save ourselves, if we want to live to save this nation, it is better that we give the Prime Minister the true stories that we know. (*Applause.*) It is better that we explain to the Prime Minister what the feelings of the people are. (*Interjections: You forgot what you said before.*) Mr Speaker, Sir, what the Members are saying...(*Interjections.*) I have sung Kamuzu No.1. I have sung that Kamuzu is the only one in this country. I have not forgotten. Even now, I still say so that he is the Prime Minister, he is the leader because that is what I believe. (*Interjection: I do not.*) He struggled and I followed him as one of the people who struggled with him and, even now, I say I will be with him because of the duty of the nation, who has taught us all to do something if we are able to do it. It is really sudden to hear what my colleagues here are saying today. (*Interjection: We are not surprised.*) I am very surprised to hear of my name being mentioned in this House the way it is being mentioned. Not being mentioned as it used to be, but being mentioned as Rose who is working against the Ngwazi. (*Interjection: Your fault.*) How can I do that today? Because I went to address the women as usual, then I am told that I went to organise against the Ngwazi because of the tickey. (*Interjection: How many times have you tried before?*) I do not think really, the one who is trying to speak knows what he is talking about...(*Interjection: I know.*)...and it is this day that I am exposed to such a lie, whether it is meant to be a lie or not...

People have given the information to the Prime Minister, the information which is not true, so that they can get this seat where I am sitting. (*Laughter.*) And this is the truth. If the people in the constituency, in one constituency are complaining, does it mean one should not bring it up? I do not go to my constituency to explain to the people about the tickies, that they should not accept going to the hospital with the tickey. Even today, if people want to say the truth, even if someone can be brought up to say or even if someone from my constituency today and say, "What did Mrs Chibambo say, what did Rose tell you? Did she speak to you about the tickey?"

Let those people speak for themselves. Even the women in Rumpi, they will say what was said by me. Even the women in Blantyre. I addressed another meeting in Blantyre. I addressed a meeting at Port Herald. I didn't mention anything about a tickey. And I have never ever uttered a word about the Prime Minister at any time, anywhere, and I am disgusted to hear that the information that has reached the Prime Minister is to say that Rose, Mrs Chibambo, has been working against the Prime Minister and the Government. It is a thing which I do not understand.

Above: Chibambo Family Portrait, 1963. From left to right: daughter Gadi, husband Edwin, son Roy, Rose carrying Phumile, daughter Royce (standing next to Roy at back), daughter Khataza and daughter Malibase (next to Rose at the front) (courtesy of The Rose L Chibambo Trust)

Below: Chibambo Family Portrait, Zambia, January 1968. From left to right: daughter Gadi, Edwin, son Roy, Rose, daughter Phumile (courtesy of The Rose L Chibambo Trust)

Above: Old Parliament Building, Zomba. It was last used in 1994. Then Parliament was moved to the capital city Lilongwe when democracy returned to Malawi (Malawi National Records & Archives Services)

Below left: Rose Chibambo on the money (courtesy of Numis Collection)

Below right: Portrait of Rose Chibambo in later life, 15 September 2005 (courtesy of Rose L. Chibambo Trust)

Chapter 15

Leaving Familiar Spaces
1964–1965

Well, after my dismissal, I packed up everything and went to Chiradzulu to be a good housewife. My husband was district commissioner of Chiradzulu at the time. We had sent the older children, Roy, Royce, Malibase and Khataza, to my mother and to my in-laws. We were with Gadi and Phumile, who were still under the age of ten.

Later, I learnt that the governor had talked to Banda, who had apparently said that everyone could come back to cabinet, except for Kanyama. The chief secretary of cabinet, Mr Peter Youens, invited Ching'oli to come and discuss the issue with Dr Banda.

Ching'oli refused to return to cabinet without Kanyama. As a result of that disagreement, Ching'oli was beaten up by guards at the prime minister's residence. The Chief Secretary had to intervene. Chirwa was nursed by Lady Jones.

This was not something I saw; as I said, I was not in Zomba or Blantyre at the time.

At one point we got a call from the government offices, saying, 'You are being transferred to Kasungu.'

I was suspicious; there was something a bit sudden about the transfer. I called the Cabinet Office and told them that my husband would not be going anywhere. I explained that this was according to doctor's instructions.

We stayed on. We were still at Chiradzulu. As soon as my husband had left for work, the Young Pioneers would come. I would stand there and look at them.

'We have instructions that whenever we see a rebel minister we should not be afraid to do anything with you. But we are afraid of God. It is you who used to tell us that we should obey our leaders.'

We were visited four times by the Malawi Young Pioneers, and the message was the same. These were people we had trained after the Ghanaian model, so that they should have vocational training. In fact, I had been in the group that had gone to Ghana to learn more about how to train the Young Pioneers. They had been taught many skills including carpentry. Yet here they were, being told to do 'whatever they wanted to do.'

Later, we were transferred to Mwanza. But you know, despite the transfer, there was no house for us to live in; there was already a DC in Mwanza. We were accommodated at Mwanza Inn. We stayed there for two weeks.

Later on, the DC who had been staying in the house moved from the area to Blantyre. The Young Pioneers came to Mwanza, entered the house. They had come from the Pioneer base at Nasawa, and they said the same thing that had been said by the group at Chiradzulu. These ones came to Mwanza twice. There was even a Jeep which came with some people who were quite aggressive in their speech.

After having been in Mwanza for a month and a half, we were told that we were being transferred to Blantyre. My husband told me that this time around, we would have to go to find our own house in Blantyre. I was surprised, because normally they should have given us a house.

All the same, he found a small house at Kanjedza. We packed up everything; a suitcase, and my husband's clothes were put in the car. My clothes were put in the lorry they had sent us.

I instructed the lorry driver, 'If you don't know where to drop these, drop them at Qabaniso Chibambo's house.'

The lorry left that day. Our plan was to follow the next day.

But then before we left Mwanza, the senior DC, Mr Walker, came from Blantyre to meet us. We were ready to move, but he told us that instead of moving to the house, we would first of all be accommodated in a hotel or that we should wait for further instructions from Zomba.

By this time, we were becoming uneasy over the way we kept being moved from place to place. We started off for Blantyre.

So, anyway, we started off, but then we reached a junction. We asked ourselves if we should really go to Blantyre. We remembered what people in Mwanza had been saying to us, telling us it would be better if we left the country as many others had done, *'Chokani muzipita kumene apita anzanu.'* ('Leave, go where your friends have gone.') The people in Mwanza had been very kind to us. As we talked, Walker followed us to the junction. He asked us why we had stopped.

I said, 'Leave us alone. We don't know what to do; we were born and grew up in Malawi.'

He said, 'You'd better go to Blantyre. Otherwise I will lose my job.'

'Leave us alone. Don't have our blood on your hands.'

He asked us to accompany him. He left in such a powerful way. *Fumbi kobo!* (Leaving dust in his wake!). Heading for Blantyre.

We made a split decision. Drove just as quickly as he had done, but in a different direction. We headed for Zobwe, the border. How we got through Mozambique border,

I shall never know, but we managed. Got to Tete. We were heading for Zimbabwe but could not make it, it was late in the evening, and the people at the border had knocked off.

We slept at an inn. I had never seen a place like that; so dirty. The water was full of mud. We could not sleep, we just sat through the night, worrying, thinking.

Later, we left the place and went into our car. In the morning, we went through Nyamapanda Border Post. We travelled until we got to Harare. But there was another problem; where would we stay? We had been lucky at the different border posts, but if we stayed at a hotel in Harare, Kamuzu would surely find out. After all, Kamuzu was friends with Ian Smith, who would be happy about this crisis. What could we do?

We were later able to find accommodation at the clinic of Dr Malkias, who was Greek. We spent a day in Harare, then left for Lusaka. I remember we reached Zambezi Bridge, between Zambia and Zimbabwe. We were cleared on the Zimbabwe side. When we entered the Zambia side, however, my husband and children were cleared; I wasn't. They said it was because I had a federal passport, not the new Malawian passport.

I was quite exhausted by this time. Was I going to be turned back now, after all we had been through? No, it could not be possible. I decided to pull rank, even though I was no longer Parliamentary Secretary.

'Give me the Minister for Home Affairs. If you mention me to him, he will know who I am.'

A few minutes later, the gate was opened for us. Oh, the relief! We drove and got to Lusaka. We arrived at Lusaka Hotel. Mr Mkwaila was there and so was Mr Katola.

We kept asking ourselves how long we would stay in a hotel.

Mr Chibambo had a distant relative, Mr Nyirenda. Mr Nyirenda was married to a daughter of my husband's cousin. When a message was sent to Mr Nyirenda, he came not really knowing whom he would meet, but correctly assuming that we were his wife's relatives.

He was very helpful, and we lived with him and his family for quite some time until we could find a place of our own.

The Host Countries: Zambia and Tanzania

Why did the former ministers, Augustine Bwanausi, Yatuta Chisiza, Willie Chokani, Orton Chirwa, Rose Chibambo and Kanyama Chiume, escape to Zambia and Tanzania? Even though Malawi shares borders with both countries, this was not the only deciding factor. Tanzania and Zambia had a history of offering asylum to political exiles. Zambia, in particular, had been the home of many African National Congress members from South Africa during the Apartheid struggle. Besides Kamuzu Banda's foreign policy of supporting the Apartheid South African government and Portuguese rule in Mozambique did not endear him to his neighbours, even though he had gained respect for his role in the fight against the Federation. Johann Müller reports that Zambia and Tanzania's antagonism towards Malawi was quite strong, took a 'long time to repair' and was visible in regional politics. For example,

> Shortly after the formation of the African Liberation Committee, it was proposed Malawi should join. Tanzania's President Nyerere, however, threatened to leave the committee if Malawi joined. Consequently, Malawi retreated.[i]

Against this backdrop, it was easy for the two countries to harbour those fleeing Malawi on political grounds. If relations had not been particularly warm before the Cabinet Crisis, they became remarkably chilly when Banda learned that the former ministers had been welcomed in Zambia and Tanzania. Baker writes about a speech Banda made subsequently with reference to Tanzania; he declared that he would invade any country that allowed itself to be used as a rebel base, 'to make sure that the invasion is not repeated.'[ii]

Later on, in 1967, President Kenneth Kaunda of Zambia wrote a conciliatory letter to Banda, explaining the country's position on the former ministers. Banda's response showed that he still did not completely trust Zambia as far as the ministers were concerned:

> On the question of ex-ministers from Malawi being granted asylum there, I am glad to hear what you say, namely, that "ever since they arrived in Zambia, it was made clear to them that they would be in Zambia as long as they did not engage in any subversive activities against their country of origin, Malawi."
>
> But whether you personally or your Government know it or not, the truth is that these ex-ministers...have been from the time they entered Zambia, actively engaged in subversive activities against the Government

of this country. Not only have they been holding meetings at night, but also they have constantly been sending subversive circulars into Malawi from Zambia. And the circulars they send are not only subversive but also scurrilous, scandalous and libelous. The source of the circulars is of course Dar es Salaam...[iii]

Chapter 16

Life Away from Home
1965–1994

LIFE AWAY FROM HOME

I remember how it used to pain me that we had been the first to get independent, but things had gone wrong for us. In Zambia, there was more openness than what we had left at home. Zambian politics seemed to be heading in a better direction than had been the case with us.

And contact with people at home?

It was minimal, because we also had to think of them, as we might get them into trouble. It was really painful, because, in the rush to get out, we had not managed to take all our children with us. As I had said before, we only managed to take the last two, Gadi and Phumile. Whenever we thought about those remaining, no... It was painful.

Later on, we learned that our son, Roy, had been imprisoned for trying to contact 'rebels' as we were known. My mother also spent some time in prison as part of the backlash.

We slowly tried to adjust. The Zambians were quite welcoming; we were able to make friends. However, our own people tended to keep to themselves.

Maybe it was fear, I don't know. All I know is that we—those of us in exile—would go to the homes of Malawians, and every time you would hear something like, 'Oh, you have come just as we were about to leave for such-and-such a place.' They would not say it directly, but you could tell they were avoiding you. They were afraid of being called rebels or of associating with those of us known as rebels.

There were therefore times when one could feel lonely, and for me, this was especially the case after my husband died in 1968. He had been ill in Zambia, but sometimes I just feel that the sadness he felt when he remembered everything that had happened to the family just made him feel worse. Oh, it was a terrible, terrible time.

The Zambian government actually offered us help in arranging for a burial in Malawi, but the Malawian government refused. A 'rebel' would not be buried on Malawian soil. You know, from the start, my husband had sacrificed a lot for us. When we were in Malawi, he was a great source of support, especially when it came to organisation in politics. Most of the time I was away from home, and the children used to stay with my husband, and he did sacrifice a lot. He never complained, he always encouraged me: 'Carry on. We want our country to be free.'

During our time in Malawi, he had been a civil servant. His brother, BaQabaniso, had been locked up in prison because of politics, and later on he was exiled, sent to exile in Port Herald, now Nsanje. As a result of arrests, such as those of BaQabaniso, who had also been a government employee, no civil servant was allowed to do politics. So my husband was just the one now taking care of the children. And in most cases, he did not eat what I cooked because I was always out, organising.

He was a very wonderful man and he encouraged me so much. Without his encouragement, I would never have done politics in Malawi. Much as I loved it, I managed because I had his support. Definitely.

And even during the time of exile, we went to exile together. He said, 'What has happened to my wife has happened to me too, because we are one.' He was a wonderful husband. Oh, very loving.

But then, after you left, going to Zambia, others to Tanzania and so on, did you ever meet again as a group?

Mmm. Not all of us together. But others in Tanzania, they used to meet; they would meet and discuss things. And we would also get the idea that, 'Oh, our friends, this is what they are saying.'

But we in Zambia rarely met, especially in regard to politics. There was our family, and then there was Chokani and late Bwanausi. I remember there was one time, and this was the time after my husband had died, when my friends came. They came saying that we should go and have a meeting in Kitwe. It was me, Bwanausi and Chokani. Now at this time, Chokani was based in Ndola, Bwanausi in Kabwe, I was in Lusaka. But we had our friends who were now part of us, like Mr Jonga, then Mr Ndovi and Mr Chapinga. I was working, so they came and said, 'We are supposed to be going to this place—Kitwe—for a meeting.'

So with me, I said, 'Ah, I don't think I can come.'

At that time, I was still in the mourning period and I could not leave my children alone, especially now that I was in a foreign land. I had nobody to leave the children with. So it was not very easy for me to go and join them.

So they said, 'Alright. Then we are going.' The people who came to talk to me about it were Mr Chapinga and Mr Jonga. Then off they went. They picked up Augustine Bwanausi. And Mr Chaponda was also supposed to be with them, Lawson was his name. He was supposed to be with them, but he refused, I don't know for what reasons. Then they went as far as Ndola; they asked Chokani, they said, 'Well, now it is time to go to Kitwe, where we are supposed to be holding a meeting.'

I understand Chokani said, 'Well, you can go ahead. I will follow you later.'

So the four of them—Bwanausi, Jonga, Chapinga, Mr Matiya—and then Ndovi went. They were driving in one car, and this was the time when they died. They died in a road accident. It was terrible. It left us with so many questions, and we were almost split.

Uhm, we never...we did not really sit together and say, 'Let us organise a meeting. And address people.' Of course, wherever we would find ourselves, politics was the subject. At the same time, we were infiltrated.

Some of our friends, who were pretending to be part of the refugee group, were spies. They pretended to be in exile; these were people that we knew, but most of them were spies. So sometimes you were better off on your own.

I met Yatuta; he had come to Zambia. It was really a brief meeting and he talked about his plans to go back to Malawi. Little did I know that would be the last time I talked to him; he would later go to Malawi and would be killed by government soldiers. There was also a time when I visited his wife in Tanzania. Mrs Chisiza was a sister to me and she had managed to live with her sons in Tanzania after the murder of Yatuta. We kept in touch and encouraged each other as we were both widowed very early in our marriages.

My other widowed Malawian sisters and I were close, some closer than others. We were in a similar situation; our husbands having passed away in Zambia, we as women had to be able to raise our children in a foreign country. One of our sisters moved back to her motherland to raise her children. We survived and we raised our children to never forget.

How did you spend your days?

I was engaged in a number of church activities; my background as someone who had been born in a Christian family helped me. But I also worked.

My first job was at a shop; it was run by Boers. It reminded me so much of the fight for independence, the State of Emergency…so I left. I then had another job at an Asian shop. We were on good terms there, and I liked the job. However, I later had the chance to work for a law firm, Shamwana and Company. But then the owner was arrested in 1980; they said he was trying to oust Kaunda's government.

I couldn't believe it. I said to myself, 'No! Why? Why is this happening to me again… being caught in a web of accusations?'

After his arrest, his partner worked at the company. He didn't do quite a good job, and there was a time when the Law Commission came to investigate him. They asked for my opinion, which I was quite happy to give. Needless to say, he wasn't happy with me, but he didn't fire me. I worked at that company for a very long time.

So that's how life was for us in Zambia. We spent a long time there.

The languages were similar to those at home, Nyanja and Tumbuka. The food was also similar. But there were of course differences; after all, these are two different countries. I remember one thing that struck me at the time I arrived was the haircut sported by young men; this was in the sixties. They used to shave off the head and leave just a patch of hair at the centre; this was something I had never seen before in Malawi.

I was there until the nineties when I got back home. The children had grown up; Gadi and Phumile were now based in the States and Malibase was in the UK. Khataza was in Blantyre. Royce was married and living in Mzimba. Many years later, Roy had also come to Zambia; he was an adult at this time. It was still difficult to get news about my children in Malawi, but there were times when I managed to do this. I would get communication, and I would also try to send news when I thought this was possible. There were times when I would go to visit Gadi and Phumile, but I still could not be sure of the situation in Malawi, especially when I thought of what my family had been through.

A Daughter's Memories

After an interview with Rose Chibambo at Chimaliro, Mzuzu, in 2013, I asked her if there was any member of the family who would feel free to speak to me. She immediately gave me Mrs Mlenje's phone number. I phoned Mrs Mlenje and we arranged to meet in Blantyre. When we finally met in February 2013, she shared insights into some of her experiences both during colonial rule and after her parents' exile.

Barbara Khataza Mlenje's Account

I'm Mrs Rose Chibambo's third born daughter. The name Khataza means *masuzgo* and the name Barbara means a stranger. The name Barbara was given to me by my father and Khataza was given to me by my grandmother.

I was born on 9th of March 1956, in Blantyre, at Queen Elizabeth Hospital. During my childhood, we were afraid of whites; they were the ones ruling the country. The whites thought Malawians were sleepy, but we could see mum. She would start off in the morning, organising meetings, but she was always there for us. And dad was with Works[22] then. He was a very quiet gentleman; I still remember his face.

When I was young, I used to suck my lip, and I remember my mum would buy me sweets so that I could break the habit. (*Laughs.*) She used to buy us nice clothes because she would travel to the UK. She would make sure we had taken breakfast before we left for school.

And then she just said that myself and Catherine—Malibase—we're going to stay with her mother. We didn't know anything. And our brother, Roy, and Royce Elizabeth—Mrs Nkunika—were at dad's home. The two of us went to Kafukule, Scott Mhango village and the other two went to Ekwendeni, Kapanda Juba Chibambo village. But we used to meet, at Christmas, on holidays...

I would help my grandmother. We would wake up around three, go to the garden during the rainy season, *kulima...basi* (cultivating maize...that's it). When I went to school *nditenge nsima ija tinadya dzulo, kukadya pa break* (I would take the *nsima* we had eaten the day before and have it during recess). (*Laughs.*) My mother had already left at this time. I was young; I didn't know anything. I didn't even know who a 'rebel' was.

But then I could hear people, *muzinyimbo amawayimba*, they would sing about her and use bad words...

---

[22] Ministry of Works.

I was an *Ingoma* singer. But sometimes they would say painful things about my mother in those songs... For me to sing that my mother was... no, I, I couldn't...I was numb. Sometimes I wanted to put my hands to my ears to block out the songs, in which they said, '*Hamba NyaZiba...*' ('Go away NyaZiba...'), but I couldn't. Not with everyone watching. It wasn't easy. By then, I didn't know what had happened, why our parents had left us in the village and taken only the last borns, Gadi and Phumile, with them. I didn't know. And when our dad died, there were a lot of mysteries that night. I saw *ma* rats together, playing, in the yard where we were...and I said, 'What's this?' I didn't understand. But you know, I was still, I was young.

Then uncle MQY (Qabaniso Chibambo) advised that I must leave Kafukule and stay with him in Mzuzu. I joined Mzuzu Government Primary School. I passed Standard Eight and I was selected to Mzimba Secondary School. I did Form One and Two, then I was selected to Mzuzu Government Secondary School. I was chosen as head girl there.

One day, I received a letter from my mum. Not a letter as such, I didn't even get it. But the police came. They called me. I only saw the letter when I got to the police station. 'What is this letter?' So I said, 'It's a birthday card.' They said, 'Why should she communicate with you?' I kept quiet. Those were difficult times. I saw a lot of youngsters being locked up. The father of a friend of mine, Sophia Mwaungulu, had also been involved in politics. She was from Karonga and was locked up in Mzuzu.

You know, they would ask you questions. They showed me a map, a very big map, which was on the wall. And the president's picture was on top, Kamuzu Banda, Ngwazi Dr Kamuzu Banda. They said, 'You are against our president, and the whole of this country from Chitipa down.' I said, 'I'm too young.'

They said, 'No, no, you can organise people.'

'How can I organise people?'

'You can organise people. You can form something like a group.'

Ihh they were shouting, and to avoid being shouted at, you kept quiet. You would stay for four hours, different people coming in, asking questions. And you don't know which room this is, they would just take you and put you in different rooms. All this happened in one day. They take you to a room, they leave you there. '*Basi tathana nawe.*' ('That's it, we're through with you.')

I didn't say anything.

Life was difficult. I didn't have a lot of money most of the time. But those who were helping me were actually *azukulu a President, ulendo wa a Mzaza* (Kamuzu's nieces, the

Mzazas.) There was Jessie Mzaza and Maureen Mzaza who became Mrs Dzanjalimodzi. They would bring me foodstuff in cartons. I don't know what they saw in me.

Life had to go on... I never knew that I could see my mum again. I saw my mum after I was already married and had two children in 1994. By then, Bakili Muluzi was the president of Malawi.

Do you see these burns? I got burnt very badly once. It was 11th of February 1987. That day, I had just got home from work; my kids were young at the time, and there was a girl who was looking after them. I was in the kitchen at night, cooking for the kids. My husband was away in South Africa at the time, on business.

A fork just fell from the frying pan, it fell down. So my son, who was two years old, wanted to pick it up. I said, 'No, don't pick it up, I'll pick it up.' So as I knelt to pick it up, there was some water for our tea—we didn't have an electric kettle. I knocked down the pot of hot water, and it just poured all over me. I collapsed.

After some time, I heard my kids crying. I said to them, 'You pray for me...' and I managed to open three doors, went out on the *khonde* and told the guard to take me to the Adventist Hospital.

I was hospitalised for three weeks. They gave me injections. My brother Ziliro—MQY's son—was there. Mum heard that I had been scalded. I think she phoned, but we couldn't talk. She said, 'How are you?' I said, 'I'm fine.' Then she cut the phone.

I don't know who told her that I was at the Adventist Hospital.

But you know, years later, long after my mother had come back from exile, I fell very ill. This was in 2011. I couldn't walk, I couldn't eat. As soon as my mother heard, she took the first available bus to Blantyre from Mzuzu and nursed me. She used to bath me and would feed me with a spoon. She would talk to me, and she would talk to God. She couldn't sleep, she was just praying.

My mother is a strong, strong, lady. She is a loving lady to everyone.

Chapter 17

The Return
1994

Chakufwa Chihana[23] played a great role in my coming back; he played a great role. He's the one who gave me assurance that all is now well at home.

He really encouraged me. He said, 'Amama, I think it's time you came back home.' In addition, I was worried because I was always thinking about my mother. I felt that if she saw other people coming back to Malawi and I was not there...I was very much torn apart.

My children in America were saying, 'Mummy, stay with us.' So I said, 'No, I can't stay with you because I have other friends at home, and my mother is there; she's still alive. I should go back and see her.'

I came back to Malawi in 1994. You know, there are some things that are so difficult to describe, and coming back was one of them. What can I say? There I was, going through the airport, the officials checking my passport, staring at me. They took quite some time on that passport, but they didn't give me any trouble.

I remember my late brother-in-law staring, 'Is it really you, Rose? Really?'

Oh, the reunion with my mother. We went home to Mzimba. You know, meeting my mother, seeing her after so many years.

And my children: Khataza, Malibase. They had all grown up. It was such an emotional time, seeing them again, just feeling fortunate that I had gotten to see them again. You know, all those years that we hadn't seen each other. It had been difficult to get news. Royce was married and living in Zambia.

My immediate concern was to build a house. The government at the time gave me some land. I have memories of sleeping in our house even before the construction had been completed; my mother was there with me. We were sleeping in this house, which had not been completed, and even then we were happy.

I also remember the bureaucracy; being given land was one thing, going to officially claim it from one office to another was quite another thing altogether. *Iiiih*, that was tough. And the other part was when I went to the Compensation Tribunal; as the widow of a civil servant, I was entitled to something, that was what had been announced. But

---

[23] Chakufwa Thom Chihana was a trade unionist and politician. He was well known for his protests against the one-party system and was arrested twice by Banda's government. The first time was from 1970 until 1977 when Amnesty International secured his release. The second time was in 1992 when he called the Malawi Congress Party a 'party of darkness and death' (Reuben Chirambo, "'The sinking cenotaph': Jack Mapanje's and Steve Chimombo's contestation of monumentalised nationalist public memories of Malawi's President Banda," *Social Dynamics* 36, no. 3 (2010): 547–564, p. 553). He was released just before the referendum of 1993. He would go on to become the founder of the Alliance for Democracy (AFORD) and to serve in Muluzi's cabinet as second vice-president. He died in 2006.

I tell you, the wait, also the idea of just being generally promised something and then it wouldn't happen. This was a different Malawi from what I had known. People in different departments made you feel as if you were a beggar and as if they were doing you a favour for the services they were supposed to give.

Before I had gone to Zambia, people used to have that feeling that they should work in order to build their country. Ah. I did not find much of that spirit when I came back.

Coming Home After Exile

The sixties, seventies and eighties saw a mass exodus of Malawians fleeing the Banda regime. Exile had initially been associated with politicians, particularly those who had fallen out with Banda during the Cabinet Crisis. But as the system became more repressive, and freedom of expression became more elusive, many people fled the country. As John Lwanda points out, the destinations were not limited to neighbouring countries. Political refugees went as far as Europe, the United States and Asia.[i]

Banda's government was based on four cornerstones: Unity, Loyalty, Obedience and Discipline. Anyone who was regarded as having flouted any of these cornerstones was arrested. In 1966, the Malawi Congress Party became the only legally recognised party in the country.[ii] Five years later, Kamuzu Banda was declared 'President for Life' by members of the Malawi Congress Party's pre-election convention.[iii] In accordance with the Decency in Dress Act of 1973, women were not allowed to wear trousers or miniskirts, and men were not allowed to wear bell-bottoms. Opposition to Banda was seen as the ultimate act of disloyalty and disobedience, and even those who were outside the country had reason to fear, especially as informers and spies were to be found both in the country and abroad.[iv]

By the early nineties, however, the political climate had begun to change, and the Malawian people were gradually questioning Banda's regime. Three factors have mostly been highlighted as contributing to this change. First was the end of the Cold War; the United States and the Soviet Union and their respective allies were no longer engaged in political and economic rivalry. The Cold War, which had commenced after the Second World War, ended in 1991 when the Soviet Union was dissolved in order to become a group of independent states. During the Cold War, the United States and countries in Western Europe had sought allies in Africa, and this meant that they mostly did not alienate African leaders by overly criticising governance. The dissolution of the Soviet Union meant that countries in the West no longer had to worry about African countries switching alliances. Countries with poor governance systems were now given conditions to change if they wished to continue receiving aid. Malawi was one of those countries that had to tread carefully after the end of the Cold War.[v]

A second factor was the improvement of international radio news.[vi] Malawians in the country were able to get wind of what was happening elsewhere, of the changes that were taking place in other countries, such as Zambia, where President Kenneth Kaunda had accepted multiparty democracy. Such awareness also helped those who were outside the country to become more outspoken in their demand for change.

A third factor was the 1992 Lenten Letter, 'Living Our Faith,' which was authored by Archbishop James Chiona, Bishops Felix Mkhori, Matthias Chimole, Alessandro Assolari, Alan Chamgwera, Gervasio Chisendera and Monsignor John Roche. The letter, which was read in Catholic churches in the country on 8 March 1992, criticised Banda's dictatorship and the government's disregard for human rights. Although the government and party machinery tried to intimidate the authors of the letter by calling them in for police questioning and issuing threats, the letter sent a strong message validating calls for change.

Subsequent voices of protest from students, mushrooming media outlets and people who felt their voices had been suppressed for a long time began to emerge. There was also, as has been indicated above, pressure from donor countries. In the wake of mass demonstrations, Banda agreed to hold a national referendum to determine if the country wanted multiparty politics. This was done, and in 1993, Malawi voted for a multiparty democracy. In May 1994, Bakili Muluzi of the United Democratic Front won the general elections and Banda conceded defeat.

It was in this climate of a changing era that some of those who had gone into exile decided to come back home. And it was during this period that Rose Chibambo made the journey back to Malawi.

Experiences of exile are as different as each individual. But there are some aspects which resonate when the discussion is about returning home from exile; the anticipation, the disillusionment, trying to fit in. Here is how Tania Ghanem, researching challenges faced by returnees, sums it up:

> ...for the majority of the refugees who had to leave their country against their will and who suddenly find themselves in a new environment, their exile presents a challenge to their relationship with their home country. It can be expected that their experience in the host country, and the way each one of them interprets it, will alter their notion of 'home' and belonging, and consequently affect their reintegration upon return.

> ...the initial period of joy starts to fade and unanticipated difficulties arise to the forefront, as the expectations invested in the country of origin during all those years of exile start to crumble. The returnee gradually realizes that the people who remained behind have changed during his/her absence and that he/she him/herself has changed.[vii]

THE RETURN

Chapter 18

A Place on the Banknote
2012

A PLACE ON THE BANKNOTE

What *was your reaction in 2012 when it was decided that your face was going to appear on the K200 note?*

I just couldn't believe it. I must say I went blank, cos it's something that I didn't expect. But when it came up, I felt very humbled. I didn't know that all that I was doing was something that some people saw to be important for the nation.

To me, I was just doing my service too, like anybody else. But to be picked up and put on that money, I just can't explain it. I really felt very much humbled about it. Even now, I sometimes even feel embarrassed. Wherever I go, those that know me, now they say, 'Oh, ndi K200.' ('Oh, that's K200.').' (*Laughs.*)

I remember the other day, I was at a shop, at Panorama, near St. Andrew's Church. I went into the shop, and there were these ladies who were selling their vegetables. And as I came out, I found that there was a crowd...but as if they were moving, but pretending to be moving, but...now they started whispering to each other.

So when I went in my car, then another lady came, *akuti*, 'Ndimwe yayi muli pa ndalama yira?' (She said, 'Aren't you the one on the money?')

I said, 'Which money?'

'That money, K200, is it not you?'

I said, 'No, we just look alike.'

(*Laughs.*) Cos I felt so embarrassed. Then they said, 'Oh, no! It's her!' I drove off. (*Laughs.*) So I just...I sometimes feel very embarrassed indeed.

But it is a wonderful feeling, definitely, to know that others appreciate the service that one rendered. I must say whoever thought of that, it's a very wonderful thing, whatever he saw...well...all I can say is that God may bless whoever that is, cos I didn't know that I deserve that.

Now, how was the photo chosen, and who decided on that particular photo?

I must say, they did not just put it on. They came, they asked me, that this was what had been decided.

Who were 'they'?

Officials from the Reserve Bank of Malawi. They asked me, they said, 'This is what has been decided,' and...it was a decision, not that they asked me. But, 'This is what has been decided.' Of course now they wanted to know, 'What do you say about it?'

But I couldn't say no. Would you say no?

No.

(*Laughs.*) As I said, I just felt very humbled that some people still think there was something that I had contributed to the nation of Malawi. Although some people may ignore it, others know the truth. Of course, when I was doing it, I wasn't doing it for fame. No, I never thought of anything, but it just came that that I thought something needed to be done here. And that's how I involved myself. So...when...of course they did ask about the pictures, if I had any photos. I showed them the photos that I had, and that photo was picked. That one is a drawing. Somebody just drew me as I was there.

Was it here or in Zambia?

No, that was done in Zambia. Somebody drew me from a photo which I had from Malawi. The photo that you see on the K200, it was snapped here in Malawi...I think that was in early 1964...between '63 and '64.

So that means what we see on the K200 note is not that painting, it's the actual photo?

It's the actual photo. It's not that painting. That painting was from the actual photo.

I've been curious about what it must have felt like to be on the K200, so you have explained how you felt.

(*Laughs.*) I feel embarrassed most of the time, I must say.

It must be interesting when sometimes you are buying things and you're looking at yourself on the currency.

(*Laughs.*) It's true. And sometimes others say, 'Ah, K200. Mundipatse a K200. Two hundred Kwacha, ni awa,' ('Give me something worth K200. She is Two Hundred Kwacha.')

So they actually call you that? Two Hundred Kwacha?

Yes. So the young people, they just take it as a joke. (*Laughs.*)

The Faces on Malawi's Banknotes

The Reserve Bank of Malawi changed the country's banknotes in 2012. For John Chilembwe and Kamuzu Banda, this was not the first time their faces had been on Malawi's money, but there were some new faces, and some new denominations:

MWK20: Inkosi ya Makhosi M'mbelwa II, Ngoni Chief, Mzimba, who was also active in opposing the Federation. He served as president of the Mombera Native Association.

MWK50: Inkosi ya Makhosi Philip Gomani II. Ngoni chief, Ntcheu, who led his people in rebelling against agricultural rules imposed by the colonial administrators. He also wrote a letter criticising the colonial government. He was arrested and later sent into exile in Thyolo, where he died.

MWK100: James Frederick Sangala. Founding member of the Nyasaland African Congress, also known as 'Pyagyusi,' the one who perseveres.

MWK200: Rose Chibambo. Founder of the Nyasaland African Congress Women's League; the only Malawian woman to have ever been on the country's currency.

MWK500: Reverend John Chilembwe. Leader of the 1915 uprising against colonial rule.

MWK1000: Dr Hastings Kamuzu Banda. First President of Malawi after independence.

In 2016, the Reserve Bank of Malawi introduced the MWK2000 with Reverend John Chilembwe's face on the obverse side.

Chapter 19

Returning to Old Routes

I benefited from my time away after we spoke last time, because I was able to read more about your history with the Women's League. And one thing that we didn't talk about last time, when we were talking about your education, was that later on, you went to night school. Can you describe that in detail?

You know, I was...what would I say? I still had the need for education. By the time I was married, I had just come out of school. And then, marriage. I was still feeling that I'm a student. (*Laughs.*) You see what I mean?

Yes.

You have just come from school, and then you are now going to be married. You feel you are still a student. So although my husband indeed was a teacher...as soon as we got married, he taught for half a year before he resigned, but I still had hunger for education. I think if I was...if I had the opportunity, like others just not to be disturbed through marriage, perhaps I could have benefited more from education, because I loved education. I loved school.

But, as you know, in those days, the people, 'Ah, you are grown up now, you better get married.' Especially him. So I got married. I had two children. Then we got transferred to Blantyre.

There was a school which was close by in Blantyre, that had not been the case in Zomba.

So I said, 'No, I should continue with my education.' I started going to night school. We used to stay at DC lines, then from there I would walk up, you know, I don't know whether they have made it as a cathedral these days... Do you know Mount Pleasant?

Yes.

Do you know where Kamuzu stayed?

No.

Kamuzu stayed along the road as we go to...whenever you are coming from the hospital as if you are going to the Catholic church.

CI.

You call it CI?

Catholic Institute.

Right there. It's where I went to night school.

At that time, we had...it was just a church at that time, and then down...I think it's where the classrooms were. But we were learning in this big block building. It's where I was going.

So how were you balancing between motherhood and studying?

During the day I would attend to my work as a housewife, as a mother, and then in the evening...I was staying with my sister. She was young, but she was quite capable, because in the evening, then she had also come back from school. I would leave her with the children and of course I used to stay with a helper, a servant, then I would leave them too. I would have organised everything during the day, and then by five o'clock, I would move on to school. Six o'clock we are in class up to half past seven, then we are out.

This issue of education is very important. In Kamuzu's speeches, especially those from 1964–65, he refers to incidents in which he offered positions to women after your dismissal from cabinet, and how these women would often say, 'Iiih, ayi, ifetu sitinaphunzire, sititha.' ('We are not educated, we will not manage.') These women were already in the Women's League. So what I wanted to find out is: when you were in the Women's League, were there issues based on class difference, education status? Did you ever experience that?

No. Not at that time. That time, it was a question of organising women to understand the issues of the nation. Why we were where we were as the Women's League, fighting for our independence.

And of course all the...I should say, because I started this in Zomba. And, as we were in Zomba, the first time I started it, of course when we said, 'Let us have our elections,' we did it. The women themselves chose me as the leader.

That feeling of not being educated did not occur at that time. We just...we were just there. Otherwise, if they had an inferiority complex in terms of education, they would never have come forward. They would have remained behind. But I took them as we were, women of Malawi. In fact, education did not come in. No. What came in was that we felt we were being enslaved. We could not go even to shopping centres, at the hospitals; we were being segregated. So that they understood it very well.

(*Sighs.*) This country, whether we are lucky or we are not lucky, ah, what are we? We don't know how to appreciate things that others have done. You see what I mean? We have that jealousy, 'Oh, why should it be so-and-so?' Now because of that, then we fail to appreciate the good things that others have done, and even to emulate, to say perhaps we should do this.

And that's why we fail even to talk about people who have done good things. And that is a disease which is eating us up. So this attitude concerning education must have occurred more, especially at the time when I had to leave. Because when I came to Blantyre, I had to start re-organising again. As I said that I was now in the main body of Nyasaland African Congress, Blantyre District. The fact that I was in the main body gave me the opportunity to talk and say, 'Please bring in ladies. They must belong to this body, because we are all fighting for the same thing. We are all the same. Men alone can never achieve anything.'

And it is true, whether they like it or not. Without the Women's League, the fight that women had put up, Malawi would not have been free as early as it was. Women were really a backbone. So that time, that element, came in, I think...it did come in. I noticed it especially after detention. At the time that I had left, now there was a gap. There was nobody who could stand up as a leader of the women, because I was out, Vera Chirwa was out, Violet Chavura was out.

This was the time after we had been arrested. We were in detention. Now...Violet Chavura. When Vera and Ching'oli came to revamp the Nyasaland African Congress, Violet Chavura was there. She was one of the most active persons and, of course, she was educated. So they worked very hard while I was still in detention.

Now, when I was in detention, I had few people, three ladies and me. Now, these three ladies, I know they didn't have...they had education, but very little.

They were with you in...

In detention, Zomba. The other one was a lady from...Thyolo, Mai Mdeza. She was an elderly lady, but very nice and humble. Very nice person. Then we had Mrs Tryness Ntenda, née Kanyashu, she was Nyakanyashu, from...she was married to a Mr Ntenda of Zomba, but she came from Usisya. She came from Nkhata Bay. And then we had Tijepani NyaGondwe, who joined us later. Tijepani NyaGondwe stayed with me. She was from Karonga. But she was pulled from Karonga, stayed with me in Blantyre, so that she could familiarise herself into politics. We wanted to coach her in politics, so that she could go and continue organising the people in Karonga.

Now we were there...because they had little education, so some of them, I could note how they would say, 'Now we are here in detention. Surely after our release, it means our independence is near.' But oh they could say, 'Hmm. And if our Parliament will be speaking English, I don't know what will happen. What will they do with all these people that have suffered so much?' You know, that sort of thing. But I never used to go into it. It had its own...you know, when you are in problems. But it didn't go too far. That was not about jealousy; they were just talking about the future.

So when we came out, now there was me, and I found Vera and Violet leading the women in a very good way. Then as soon as I was released, I joined them.

When were you released?

I was released in 1960, in March.

So you were released, and you found that these women had worked really hard to revamp the party.

Yes. They had worked very hard to revamp the party. And...ah, it had changed the name into Malawi Congress Party, because Nyasaland African Congress had been banned.

So they worked hard, and Vera and Violet had education. They would speak English frequently. And in fact, Violet was a teacher by profession. So, then there I was, but the committee that we had now in our Women's League, uhm, they had little education, they could not speak English, but they were intelligent women; they understood things.

After the crisis, when we had gone out, I don't know what was happening here. Because now the three of us had become unpopular. So there was just a vacuum, there was nobody.

The three of you as in Chavura, Vera Chirwa and yourself?

Yes. We were now out of the way. Then I remember at one stage, after we had already left the country, Dr Banda tried to send somebody that they should ask me to come back, cos the Women's League was now not functioning properly. That's what I was told. But I knew that things were not well; there was no need to come back. Even some of the good will people used to say, 'This is what they want you to do. But definitely, we don't want to be part of it, because we know you may not survive.' Because...there was...Kamuzu's name, I know...it was used, people were jealous. Jealousy was rife that...I can't just say...

People called us names; they tried to say this and that...things which were not true at all. But because they wanted to get nearer...just as you see even now, what goes on. They move from this party to another, and with all the praises that they talk...they don't really mean it...ah ah. (*Laughs.*)

Oh, I have known it, my dear. I know. And, in fact, our beginning, it's not what is going on now. It's now because there's...people see that there's dignity...you look like somebody if you are in politics, and there's money which people get now, lavishly, but during our time there was nothing, my dear. There was no car.

No ministerial car?

(*With emphasis*) No car. We used to walk; you go organising women, you're walking...

Even when you became parliamentary secretary?

I had to buy my own car. In fact, my husband got a car himself, then later on we said, 'Ah, we'd better get something, a car.' Although I—we—didn't last, my dear. They had already planned it. It was just nothing but petty jealousy.

After we had done everything for this country. Now others wanted to just have it out of nothing, and indeed, they are continuing even now.

I am one of the few who are still surviving, most of my friends are gone, but they have left families which are suffering. Who tries to attend to them? Nobody. Because it is their time. But they don't know how they came to where they are now. This is one thing: we cannot receive blessings. You have to look at where you came from. You don't have to ignore it. If you know where you came from, you will know where you are going.

But this is not the case in Malawi. And, perhaps that's why we are failing even to move forward, you know. It's now we are going to fifty years since independence, what have we achieved? We don't think about the nation as a whole, but individuals. We individually think, 'How much can I accumulate?' So I really don't know because...this was not the case when we were fighting. If we fought with a spirit of saying, 'Oh well, I should benefit,' we would never have done anything. But the thing was, 'Our people are suffering, we are suffering together with our people, let us achieve something, so that we can be known to be who we are.' But it was short-lived. When I think of, really, my colleagues that struggled together to see this country free; the two Chisizas, Chipembere, Kanyama, I was there. And then later on, some joined us, later. Then we had the Youth League, Chindongo. And most of the people whose names you hear, most of them came in after the State of Emergency. That's when many people came in.

At first, many people were afraid, thinking that those who would be in trouble would be those at the forefront. They thought those at the forefront wanted to show off.

Others had the spirit, but they didn't want to be seen that they are there. You see? So unfortunately, when the State of Emergency came, little did they know that they were actually being spotted that they had the interest in politics.

And then you told me about the reaction of the boys in class. And I started noticing that wherever you went...let's say, in the Central Body, even in the ministry, because that aspect of being the only woman continued. How did the men react? Were they a bit like the boys in your classroom?

No. Even when I was with these friends in politics, as I said, I was in the Blantyre District as a treasurer, Mikeka Mkandawire was the chairman, Hartwell Solomon was the secretary, we were just working as colleagues. There was no feeling of ah, perhaps you have done this or I did that, no.

And this is one thing that perhaps up to now, when I work with people who have not known me, they find it a bit strange that I speak freely. Even where there are men. In the party, we had Mr Makata, Lawrence Makata, we had them there, Mr Somanje...I never felt anything, my dear. I never felt...and indeed...I was just the only woman through and through but it never occurred to me that I was there as a woman. I was just one of them.

If it was contributing, we had to contribute together as people. I was around when TDT

Banda was there, I was still the only woman when he left, we carried it forward until when Dr Banda came; I was the only woman, so I never felt any strange thing. I was just one of the people.

I was reading this book by Colin Baker, it's called Revolt of the Ministers. *He suggests that, especially after Dr Banda became prime minister, it was like sometimes there was a kind of division. According to the book, you were closer to Yatuta and Chipembere was closer to Bwanausi. Did you ever notice that kind of division that you tended to side more with Yatuta, whereas Chipembere would be in the same camp with Bwanausi, so to speak?*

Uhm, no, that division, I didn't notice it myself. I only remember that we would act as a group. Because...I remember I think perhaps where Dr Banda was more annoyed.

There was a time when we were already now in the cabinet. We had visitors...before Mozambique was independent. Portuguese visitors came to Malawi and...I think it was an official visit. So we had a cocktail party for them at... Ryall's Hotel, was it? I think it was at Ryalls hotel.

So Chipembere sat, here I was, and there was Kanyama...No, Kanyama was next to Chipembere, I sat here, and Aleke Banda was here. So Dr Banda had sat somewhere and...with other people.

So when these people were being addressed, Kanyama was very jokey and sometimes you even failed to resist his jokes. So at that time, you know our friends the FRELIMO were still fighting the Portuguese. And then as we were there, I think it was Kanyama, he said, 'Ah, we're sitting here like stooges with these colonialists.' Then we were all pressed for laughter. And it was during this time that Dr Banda was talking. Chipembere had to get up because he found it difficult to contain his laughter; in the end he stood up and went out. But I know Dr Banda was not pleased with that.

But to say that we were separated in a sort of a camp, no, that I didn't notice myself. But you know, people like Baker, yes he writes things, but some of the things I don't agree with. But the book that was written by Andrew Ross; he speaks more of what we were. Baker, because he gets things from this one and that one, whereas Andrew Ross was in the country and he was quite involved with us. And during the State of Emergency, he was one of the people who used to come and visit us. They even lent me their children's pram; I was using it for my baby in prison.

Of course, sometimes, you know, where people are, you would differ in views. Especially in a political situation. There came a time when Dr Banda was actually doing this using divide and rule. He would call me, I would go to him. He would discuss issues with me, and then he would tell me, 'You'd better be careful with so-and-so', meaning one of my colleagues.

'You must be careful with so-and-so.' Automatically, I would feel that...perhaps that one comes to talk things against me to the president. And he did that to each and every one, so that we became as if we were enemies of each other. You will look at me in a certain way because he has told you that you should be careful where I'm concerned. And by the time you come out, now you'll be wondering. Even if I chat with you, you will be wondering, 'Ah, is this a friend? Should I trust him? And we had reached that stage.

If we could come back to the present now, I know you tried to start an orphanage and I'm interested in that. Is it an on-going project? What projects are you involved in at the moment?

I would say, the project of the orphanage, it's not a project in the sense that I might be earning anything out of it. That was not the aim. It is just the same feeling that perhaps drove me into politics.

When I came back, especially 2000, there was hunger and so many people really suffered. And then at the same time, we had so many orphans, some whose parents had died because of AIDS and so on. And since I was also involved with the church...I should say the first time I came, nobody knew that I was here. Then the church, which had embraced me as one of its members, took me into so many projects that they have. At one time I was incorporated in PAC, Public...whatever...which we have in Lilongwe.

Public Affairs Committee?

Was it that one? I think so. But, yes...I was also there. The church had just introduced me there when they heard...I think they had heard of gender, that when we are doing these things, ladies, too, must be involved. So CCAP Livingstonia was asked, when they were holding a meeting here of PAC. The reverend at that time was Reverend Mvula, and he asked me if I could attend that meeting together with some gentlemen.

So I agreed. I said yes. That was the first time. And then from that meeting, then Synod of Livingstonia have involved me in a number of bodies. I have been working with them in a number of bodies and I represent the Synod on a number of board meetings and so on, together with other members of the Synod. This is where I have been so much involved.

And then even on partnership, when Synod of Livingstonia became a partner with Eastern Oklahoma in the United States, I was in the first delegation that went to make that partnership. So I've been on quite a number of boards, especially related to churches. I have been on Church Development and Aid, for instance. The church has really made use of me since my arrival from Zambia.
And then lastly, they even awarded me.

That's the church?

Yes. They gave me an award.

Now, coming to the orphanage, the idea was born in 2000. That was just something that touched me. I felt that so many children were suffering, and as a result, I felt...I thought Malawi was the same Malawi that I knew. I said, 'Can't I do something, perhaps through my name? These children could be helped.'

So I went to the social welfare here in Mzuzu. And I asked them how I could help, as I really wanted to do something. So they told me at that time that almost all of the areas had been covered.

But they said there was an area in Katawa which had nobody to assist them. So if it was possible, then I could definitely help them.

So I said, 'Oh, fine.' Then I went to Katawa area. They had a committee of their own, and in this committee, cos...in those days, they used to have a certain area with a chief... *amasankhana ma chiefs wene wake momwemo* (they choose one another as chiefs in those areas). So a certain area with a chief, then the chief is sort of a chairman. He has a committee with which he works in order to assist the children.

So I approached that committee. I asked them what problems they faced and how I could assist them, if I could. So they explained to me, said, '*Inde* we have these orphans, although they are indeed within the homes with their guardians, the guardians have nothing. So if there's anything, then it would be a great help to them.'

So then I came back. (*Laughs.*) I wrote letters to all the departments in Malawi, asking for assistance. To all the hotels, the parastatals, everywhere, you name them, I sent them letters. Not one answered me. Whether they felt that I just wanted to enrich myself, I don't know. And it worried me. I had already approached those people, what was I going to do? I worried, definitely, and I prayed.

'Lord, help me. How can I solve this?'

At one point, I met my friend Violet Chavura as I said. I was telling her the dilemma that I was in. So she said, 'Oh, we were in the same dilemma. You approach this lady.' She gave me the name of a lady in Scotland, and that lady, I know her and she knows me. This was Mrs Patsy Colven. And when I wrote her telling her about our problem, she happened to be in the group of Scottish Child Survival in Malawi.
She wrote back, to say that she had approached her friends, and they would try to do something. Those are the ones who started helping us by sending us the little money they could. Then with that money, we would always buy food. After buying the food then I would take it to go and feed the children.

Is the orphanage still thriving now?

Actually, what I have been doing is, each time we receive something, then we will buy foodstuff and distribute it to them. Then we buy things, take them to the area, and I ask the committee to gather all the children. So we go there and distribute it to them all the time. But since the economy crisis all over the world, we are not getting any help anymore.

Oh, so the project is still there, but it's just that...

The project is there, but I just can't afford anything. I don't have people who can support us, and in any case, now, I just feel that...I think I'm tired. But I still feel that I should go, before December ends, I'll go and visit them and tell them the problems that are there...

So Malawians as individuals or organisations don't contribute to the project?

No, they don't. I have never had any organisations contributing apart from the group which I also work with the Prison Group. Sometimes we raise funds by making tea, coffee, and so on. So whatever remains there, like last time, they had some remaining foodstuff, so they said, 'You can give this to the children,' that was all. It's very difficult to raise funds.

I had hoped that people would be willing to assist, but no. And as it is now, they have another project next to us, to Katawa, they are the only ones who received some help from the MP from Mzuzu. And yet he was voted for Mzuzu as a whole, but he only gives it to a certain group of people.

I have noticed that you are also involved with the Ngoni Cultural Heritage. Could you tell me a few things about your involvement with the group?

In the Ngoni Heritage, we help to organise our traditional remembrance, so to say. And I and Reverend Sande, we are supposed to be...what do they call them...I should say, in most cases, we are always there. It is one of the most wonderful things and I really admire it. I love it, because Ngoni customs generally, they are very nice, and when you come to talk about respect in Ngoni, it's just wonderful. And the dancing itself, the men's dance, and the women's dance, very graceful. Oh, it's lovely.

It's just unfortunate that sometimes we don't have much time. So I'm very much involved and I love it.

You lead a very busy life, I can see.

Now I'm tired. This time I'm really tired.

And when you are not busy, what do you do in order to relax?

Uhm, I don't really have real time to relax. When I relax it means I must have been somewhere and I'm tired. (*Laughs.*) I am very much involved in the church activities; that is part of my life. I have always loved God and I feel it is...it's part of me that I should serve him. Whenever I can, I should give my services to God. So whenever there are meetings or activities concerning the church anywhere, I'm always there.

Of course, sometimes I do fail, but definitely I feel very much involved with the church, and I take it to be part of me. Yes. Uhm, the church— I should say, the Christian life— it has been part of my life ever since I was young because my mother and my father, our home, was a real Christian family. My father was a teacher by profession, but we lived a life of knowing about Christianity. And as I was growing up, many church ministers, reverends of our areas, whenever they are holding church services—because in those days they used to walk quite a distance—they would stay at our house.

Whenever there were meetings, whether it is at Njuyu, whether it is at Kafukule, they would stay at our house. Oh yes.

So I grew up. I knew that these are the church people and therefore I have to go to church, and I'm part of it. That's how I grew up. Definitely.

And who are your close friends at the moment?

(*Laughs.*) Ah. Ah *ayi*, I don't know. I just see whoever is there as my friend. Those we have been close to, we meet; those are my friends. Definitely. But I regard Violet Chavura as my friend, and Molly Zabala—Molly Bwanausi Zabala. And then Mary Bwanausi, because we have been in exile together. We grew up as sisters; we just accepted each other as people with the same problems. So we were very close, even in exile. So even here, it's just the distance that is parting us, otherwise we are very good friends.

The Rubadiris, Dr and Mrs Mkandawire are family too and we spend a lot of time together.

So as I came home, people would not associate with you if you had been in exile. They were looking at you as if you were still a rebel, as they called us, so that, in most cases, people would not be very free with you. And they couldn't believe, some of them even couldn't believe that they were seeing me. And perhaps some of them were even afraid to get closer to me that they might be...this was now when I was back here. People couldn't really believe that they were seeing me having come back. Definitely.

(*Sighs.*) I think dictatorship was too much. You know, people have been destroyed. After all that dictatorship, I don't know what people have learnt, because this type of corruption, it wasn't there in Malawi before. And people have become dishonest, people don't seem to care anymore about others, which...it wasn't there before. So you really just feel sorry; dictatorship destroys people. It does. Because sometimes they don't even trust anybody.

A Daughter's Tribute

I am Edwin and Rose Chibambo's fifth-born child. They named me Gadi. This Ngoni name means prison. My mum took me along with her to prison during the fight for our country's independence. For a young mother with a newborn baby, she was exposed to very difficult, unsuitable conditions for standing up for what was right. I salute my mum for her faith, her strength and her resilience.

Our mum told us about another woman prisoner who insisted on feeding me porridge. She would go around the back to supposedly feed me. After a few of these feeding sessions and on noticing I came back crying each time, one of the other imprisoned women decided to investigate. She discovered and told mum that I was not being fed but rather the woman was feeding herself with my porridge and possibly giving me only a spoonful! That put a stop to those feeding sessions. I thank God for all the women who were in prison with mum and all the missionaries who helped with food, clothing and moral support. It is by the grace of God we survived that ordeal.

My earliest recollection as a whole family was our last Christmas together in December 1964 in Mwanza. Soon after that my older siblings were sent up North to continue their schooling since we were transferred so often. We left Malawi early in January 1965 and my parents regretted sending their older children to the North throughout our stay in Zambia. After our dad passed away, mum was the rock that held us together even though we, as a family, were separated physically. We were in Zambia and our older siblings were in Malawi. Our family was one of the few who had the misfortune of not being able to be reunited as one. Most families who left Malawi during the crisis were helped by other family members in Malawi to reunite with their children who had been inadvertently left behind. This distance truly, deeply hurt my parents.

She made certain we never forgot where we came from, our heritage and our language. She insisted on always addressing us in ChiTumbuka and raising us in our Ngoni customs.

Mum instilled in all of us the desire to pursue an education, to always be the best you can be and to be fiercely independent. Mum herself had studied in Lusaka and achieved a Bookkeeping Certificate. When I told our mum I wanted to embark on a Doctor of Dental Surgery programme, she was very supportive. She got in touch with friends she had made over the years and with relatives who had also been scattered across the world as a result of the Cabinet Crisis in 1964. She also supported my studies with her salary as well as by selling eggs, chickens and baked goods. And our Aunt Nellie was very supportive always. As a result, I was able to study to become a dentist. As my mother's daughter, I also sought scholarships and worked while in University to alleviate the financial burden. It was a momentous day when I completed the Doctor of Dental Surgery programme and our mum participated in my graduation at Howard University in Washington DC.

I truly appreciate our mum's boldness to go where most women would not go. She was the first woman in Southern Africa to take up a Cabinet position. She was fearless in her pursuit of independence for the people of Malawi. She was courageous among her male peers and stood up for the women of Malawi so they could have a voice. Take note all politicians in Malawi, men and women! She was a deeply loving mum, though tough at times. Yet her toughness gave us strength and saw us all through challenging and hostile times. Mum embraced other children borne by other mothers in her life whom she considered her own. We are her 'dear ones,' as she would say, and we will preserve her legacy.

Eh Ziba, bakwa Sambili! I salute you, Mummy. Always loved, never forgotten.

Dr Gadi Chibambo-Smith
September 2019

***

Looking Back, Looking Forward

In November 2014, Karonga Museum celebrated ten years of existence. Rose Chibambo was one of the Living Legends honoured during the function. Lusubilo Band entertained guests, and the female vocalist, Rebecca Mwalwenje,[24] led a performance that included a vast, impressive repertoire, from jazz, gospel, and rumba to Afro-pop.

After the function, sChibambo, smiling, said, 'You know, I saw that girl's confidence, and I said to myself, that's how crazy I was, back then. There are always a few crazy ones in every age.'

---

[24] Since the performance that captivated Rose Chibambo in 2014, Rebecca Mwalwenje has gone on to forge a successful solo career. In addition to being a vocalist, she is also a guitarist and went to Norway for further training in 2015. Now back in Malawi, she also facilitates music workshops ,the most recent of which was in 2018 at the University of Malawi, Chancellor College.

RETURNING TO OLD ROUTES

Epilogue

The Last Word

THE LAST WORD

Sometimes I may not be able to follow up things properly, but that has been my life; this is how politics came about. As I said, it's not something that somebody forced me into, but I was interested to see if I could contribute. As early as that, when Malawi politics was not known to women. There's always a beginning, and that was it.

But at the same time, what pains me more now is that we have taken politics as something whereby one wants to get rich, not as something with which we want to help the needy or the poor people, to bring them to understand things, to understand their own life, how they can live. But not in the way things are moving.

You know what? I don't mind what someone says; I'm speaking about the things that I see. And I fought in order for things to be better. And when I see things going wrong now, it pains me, because I sometimes feel, was it worth fighting for? Sleeping on the floor in the prisons, for the sake of our country to be free.

You see, people, so many people, we fought for higher education in Malawi. Now we have managed to get education. And now that education, we're destroying it. You cannot choose a student because he or she is from your area. That is totally wrong, because those students belong to the country. We should choose students according to merit; who has qualified where, let him go and do what he can do better, because when he comes back, he will serve this very nation, no matter which part of the country he comes from. These are our children. So if we get the brilliant children, we spend more money on them, so that they can come back and help to develop the country, so much the better for us all. But then we try to mix things, which is totally wrong.

Because if we had that spirit at the time we were fighting, this country would never have been free. Not at all. The idea was that this is our nation, no matter where we come from.

I didn't start politics in the North. No. It was in Zomba where I learnt politics. And I organised the people in Zomba and we were all just up together. And that's how it should be.

Now from that time, we got independent. People have gone...we have trained people, 'Oh, let us send our children here. Oh, let them learn this.' Engineers in different fields, doctors. But here we are. We are in the same situation. What has gone wrong? Where are the educated people that Malawi has spent all the money on? Well, you spend in order to gain, don't you? Now what are we gaining? What has gone wrong? Where is the educated class? What are they doing? They have to do something, because they have that education. Don't just keep it to yourself.

You have actually to impart it, no matter which area you are sharing it with. You should have that feeling to say, 'Ah, I am this. I think this can be done in such-such an area.'

Don't choose to say, 'Because this cannot grow here, or because I cannot do this here in my home, therefore I can't do it, then I'll just keep quiet.' No, no. That's not fair. Wherever you think, 'This knowledge, I can pour it there,' take it there. It is within Malawi, it is for Malawi. It's not for anybody else. So I really feel very sad, my dear, when I see things in the way they go wrong.

Kuti where are all those educated people? That's why I said earlier, I think dictatorship destroys people. Perhaps some of them have the knowledge but they just say, 'Ah, if I say this, ah, I will be told that I'm wrong.' Then you keep quiet. No! Don't keep quiet. Speak and point out where the mistakes are. Others will know. Even if someone may oppose you strongly, but if they are opposing you on something which is true, you will always achieve something.

So it's up to you young people; this is the country, we got it for you. I'm speaking, it's Rose here talking, I'm still around, I know what this nation was, and where we have brought it from. It is really for you. Either you destroy it or you save it.

THE LAST WORD

Glossary

In the glossary below, where languages are not spelled out, different letters denote the following languages: A represents Afrikaans terms, C represents ChiChewa terms, N represents ChiNgoni terms, T represents ChiTumbuka terms, and Z represents isiZulu terms.

Agogo	C, T	Grandparent
Amama	C, T	Mother
Ankhoswe	C	Marriage counsellors, responsible for the affairs of marriage
Ayi	C	No, and not
Ba	T	Prefix used to show respect, as in BaQabaniso
Bafana	N	Young boys
Basirikalis	T	Soldiers
Borodi	T	Preliminary education system which involved writing on the ground, preparing the pupil for the time s/he would start using notebooks
CCAP		Church of Central Africa Presbyterian
Chigayo/zi-	C	Maize mill/s
DC		District Commissioner
FRELIMO		*Frente de Libertação de Moçambique*, Mozambique Liberation Front
Fuko	C, N	Snuff box
Gawa	C	Share
(Wachi)gulumuntira	C	Blind, Uninitiated
HHI		Henry Henderson Institute
Incwala	N	Ritual of kingship among the Ngoni
Inde	C	Yes
Inkosi	N	Chief
Iwe	C, T	You
Izinduna	N	Chief's ministers
Ka	C, T	Prefix used to refer to something small
Kasepuka na ka Sungwana	T	A little boy and a little girl
Katundu	C, T	Luggage
Khonde	C	Veranda
Kraal	A	Enclosure for cattle, sheep or goats
Kuboola	C	To pierce, piercing
Kuti	C, T	That
Kwawoko	C	At their home
Lobola	N, T	Dowry
Masuku	C	Fruit of the msuku (wild loquat, *Uapaca Kirkiana*)

GLOSSARY

Masuzgo	T	Problems
Mathenga	N	Those entrusted with the duty of formally asking for a girl's hand in marriage
Mathuli na misi	T	Mortar and pestle
Mchoma	N, T	Traditional dance
MCP		Malawi Congress Party
Mfecane	Z	The Great Trek
Mgaiwa	C, T	Unrefined maize flour
Mipini	C, T	Adzes
MP		Member of Parliament
Mphepete	C	Edge
Mphepo	C, T	Wind
Mthimba	N, T	Marriage ceremony
Mutu bii!	C	Dark-skinned person
Mxamati	N	Small knife
NAC		Nyasaland African Congress
Nawo	C, T	They too
Ndiwo	C, T	Relish
Ndora	T	Dance
Ngoma/Ingoma	N	Ngoni dance
Ngwazi	C	Big strong man
Ngwembe	N	Wooden plate
Nsima	C, T	Thick maize porridge eaten with relish
Nyanga ya njobvu	C	Elephant tusk
PAC		Public Affairs Committee
Palibe njira	C	No through road
PWD		Public Works Department
Salu/Nsalu	N, T	Clothing material
Ufa	C	Maize flour
Uko	C, T	There
Umsindo	N	Initiation ceremony in preparation for marriage
Vikono	N, T	Iron bracelets
Vidokoni	N, T	Part of Tumbuka and Ngoni folklore; stories
Vyakulimira	T	Hoes
Wena	N, Z	You
Wosesa	C	Sweeper

Notes

Introduction
[i] Jessie Kabwila, Timwa Lipenga and Hendrina Kachapila-Mazizwa, "Remembering Ourselves: Conversations with Malawian Women," (Project Proposal) (2011).

1 Mzimba, the Early Days (1920s–1940s)
[i] Desmond Dudwa Phiri, "Some notes on the Ngoni Clans of Malawi and the Ngoni Celebrations at Mabili of September, 2002," *The Society of Malawi Journal* 55, no. 2 (2002): 65–71 (p. 66).
[ii] TJ Thompson, "The Origins, Migration and Settlement of the Northern Ngoni," *The Society of Malawi Journal* 34, no. 1 (1981): 6–35 (p. 11).
[iii] "Besselian Elements: Total Solar Eclipse of 1835, November 20," National Aeronautics and Space Administration, accessed 25 July 2019, http://eclipse.gsfc.nasa.gov/SEsearch/SEsearchmap.php?Ecl=18351120.
[iv] John McCracken, *Politics and Christianity in Malawi, 1875–1940* (Blantyre: Christian Literature Association of Malawi, 2000), p. 149.
[v] Al Mtenje and Boston Soko, "Oral Traditions and Language among the Ngoni," *Journal of Humanities* 12 (1998): 1–18, (p. 8).
[vi] Special Absalom, "Malawi Senior Chiefs Detained for Wearing Animal Skins and Ivory Bangles," *The Maravi Post*, 27 February 2018, accessed 18 September 2019, http://www.maravipost.com/malawi-senior-ngoni-chiefs-detained-wearing-animal-skins-ivory-bangles/.
[vii] Mtenje and Soko, "Oral Traditions," (pp. 1–2).

2 Moving into Family Roles (1920–1940s)
[i] Margaret Read, "Moral Code of the Ngoni and their Former Military State," *Africa: Journal of the International Institute of African Languages and Cultures* XI, no. 1 (1938): 8–10.
[ii] Desmond Dudwa Phiri, "Some notes on the Ngoni Clans of Malawi and the Ngoni Celebrations at Mabili of September, 2002," *The Society of Malawi Journal* 55, no. 2 (2002): 65–71 (p. 70).
[iii] Read, "Moral Code," p. 9.

3 The Night Walk (1930s–1940s)
[i] Report by MJ Crow, Geological Survey, Malawi, 1982, in *Catalogue of Meteorites*, Cambridge: Cambridge University Press, (Reprint, 2001), p. 348.
[ii] MJ Crow, "Malawi Meteorites: 1899–1981," *The Society of Malawi Journal* 36, no. 1 (1983): 16–32 (p. 21).

4 Remembering Recreation (1930s–1940s)

[i] TJ Thompson, *Christianity in Northern Malaŵi: Donald Fraser's Missionary Methods and Ngoni Culture* (Leiden, New York, Cologne: Brill, 1995), p. 90.
[ii] Lupenga Mphande, "Ngoni Praise Poetry and the Nguni Diaspora," *Research in African Literatures* 24, no. 4 (1993): 99–122 (p. 108).
[iii] Margaret Read, "Songs of the Ngoni People," *Bantu Studies* 11, no. 1 (1937): 1–35 (p. 6). Note: Read's translations tend to use the archaic forms 'thee' and 'thou.'

5 Duties in the Kitchen and Maize Field (1930s and 1940s)

[i] John McCracken, *A History of Malawi: 1859–1966* (Suffolk: James Currey 2012), p. 179.
[ii] John McCracken, *A History*, p. 180.
[iii] Ibid.
[iv] Donald Fraser stated that the Ngoni 'hoed not, nor did they spin' (Fraser, *The Autobiography of an African*, London, 1925, as cited by TJ Thompson, "The Origins, Migration and Settlement of the Northern Ngoni," *The Society of Malawi Journal* 4, no. 1 (1981): 6–35 (p. 23).
[v] TJ Thompson, "The Origins," p. 23.

6 Travelling with Childhood Companions (1930s–1940s)

[i] Boston Soko, interview by Timwa Lipenga, Kaning'ina, Mzuzu, 9 October 2014.
[ii] Margaret Read, *Children of their Fathers: Growing Up Among the Ngoni of Nyasaland*, (New Haven: Yale University Press 1960), pp. 89–90.
[iii] D. Gordon Lancaster, "Tentative Chronology of the Ngoni, Genealogy of their Chiefs, and Notes," *The Journal of the Royal Anthropological Institute of Great Britain and Ireland* 67 (1937): 77–90 (p. 81).

7 In Search of Education (1930s–1940s)

[i] John McCracken, *A History of Malawi: 1859–1966* (Suffolk: James Currey 2012), p. 113.
[ii] Isaac Lamba, *Contradictions in Post-War Education Policy Formulation and Application in Colonial Malawi, 1945–1961* (Zomba: Kachere, 2010), p. 124.

8 From the Classroom to Courtship (1940s)

[i] McCracken, John. *Politics and Christianity in Malawi: The Impact of the Livingstonia Mission in the Northern Province.* (Blantyre: Christian Literature Association in

Malawi, 2000), p. 297.
[ii] Kenneth Ross, *Christianity in Malawi: A Source Book*. (Zomba and Gweru: Kachere Press, Mambo Press, 1996), p. 157.
[iii] Ross, *Christianity in Malawi*, p. 155.
[iv] MNA 47/LIM/3/17 p. 331, in Ross, *Christianity in Malawi*, p. 155.

9 Wedding Preparations and Marriage (1947)

[i] Margaret Read, "Songs of the Ngoni People (Lullabies, Umsindo and Mthimba Songs)," published on 'The Ngoni People of Africa' website, original text from 1937, accessed 7 August 2019 https://allthingsngoni.wordpress.com/2010/08/15/songs-of-the-ngoni-people-lullabies-umsindo-and-mthimba-songs/.
[ii] Ibid.
[iii] Ibid.

10 Moving into Political Spaces (1950s)

[i] Owen JM Kalinga, *Historical Dictionary of Malawi* (Lanham, Toronto, Plymouth: The Scarecrow Press, 2012), p.160.
[ii] Ibid.
[iii] Kalinga, *Historical Dictionary*, p. 161.
[iv] Kalinga, "Resistance, Politics of Protest, and Mass Nationalism in Colonial Malawi, 1950–1960: A Reconsideration," *Cahiers d'Études Africaines* 36, no. 143 (1996): p. 448.
[v] Carl Rosenberg Junior, "The Federation of Rhodesia and Nyasaland: Problems of Democractic Government," *Annals of the American Academy of Political Science* 306: Africa and the Western World (1956): p. 98.
[vi] Ibid.
[vii] Elias Mtepuka, "Central African Federation: 1. The Attack," *Africa South* (1957): p. 73.
[viii] "Why be shy about the Federal Flag?" *The Nyasaland Times*, 17 October 1958.
[ix] Ibid.
[x] John McCracken, *A History of Malawi: 1859–1966* (Suffolk: James Currey 2012), p. 331.
[xi] "Queen Honours Loyalty and Service," *The Nyasaland Times*, 16 June 1959.

11 Out with the Old, in with the New (1950s)

[i] Joey Power, *Political Culture and Nationalism in Malawi: Building Kwacha* (Rochester: University of Rochester Press 2010), p. 204.
[ii] John McCracken, *A History of Malawi: 1859–1966* (Suffolk: James Currey 2012), p. 337

iii Andrew Ross, *Colonialism to Cabinet Crisis: A Political History of Malawi* (Zomba: Kachere Press 2009), p. 105.
iv McCracken, A History, p. 344, *Power, Political Culture*, p. 126, Ross, *Colonialism to Cabinet*, p. 98.
v See *Power, Political Culture*, p. 128.
vi *Power, Political Culture*, p. 126.
vii Ross, *Colonialism to Cabinet*, p. 106.
viii McCracken, *A History*, p. 345.
ix Ross, *Colonialism to Cabinet*, p. 108.
x *Power, Political Culture*, p. 127.
xi Ross, *Colonialism to Cabinet*, p. 159.

12 The Meeting in the Bush and Time in Prison (1959–1960)

i Philip Murphy, "A Police State? The Nyasaland Emergency and Colonial Intelligence," *Journal of Southern African Studies* 36, no. 4 (2010): 765–780 (p. 766).
ii Ibid.
iii Murphy, "A Police State?" p. 766.
iv Murphy, "A Police State?" p. 771.
v Colin Baker, *State of Emergency: Crisis in Central Africa, Nyasaland 1959–1960* (London and New York: Tauris and Academic Studies, 1997).
vi Brian Simpson, "The Devlin Commission (1959): Colonialism, Emergencies, and the Rule of Law," *Oxford Journal of Legal Studies* 22, no. 1 (2002): 17–52 (p. 20).
vii Paul Chiudza Banda and Gift Wasambo Kayira, "The 1959 State of Emergency in Nyasaland: Process and Political Implications," *The Society of Malawi Journal* 65, no. 2 (2012): 1–19 (p. 10).
viii "Another of the Four,' *Nyasaland Times*, Friday, 3 April 1959.
ix "British seize African mother after childbirth," *Jet* 15.24, 16 April 1959.
x Zondiwe Mbano, interview with Timwa Lipenga, Zomba, September 2012.

13 The Role of Music and Dance in Politics

i John McCracken, *A History of Malawi: 1859–1966* (Suffolk: James Currey 2012), p. 372.
ii John McCracken, *A History*, p. 369.
iii Ibid.
iv Colin Cameron, e-mail response to questionnaire, 12 March 2013.
v Speech made by the Prime Minister of Malawi, Ngwazi Dr H Kamuzu Banda at the State Luncheon on 5 July 1964. Press release no. 1043/64.
vi Joey Power, *Political Culture and Nationalism in Malawi: Building Kwacha*

(Rochester: University of Rochester Press 2010), p. 182. Power also comments on the way in which the Prime Minister's Office was particular about the wording of Chibambo's duties, stating that she was there to "assist," as opposed to "advising" the Prime Minister in the implementation of his plans.
[vii] Dunduzu Kaluli Chisiza, "Africa: What Lies Ahead" *Indian Council for Africa* (1962): p. 42.

14 The Cabinet Crisis (1964)
[i] Speech by Banda, Legislative Council Proceedings, 28 November 1961, p. 101 (in McCracken, *A History of Malawi*, pp. 403–404).
[ii] McCracken, *A History*, p. 404.
[iii] McCracken, *A History*, p. 431.
[iv] McCracken, *A History*, p. 432.
[v] From Proceedings of Parliament, 1964–1965 "Second Meeting—First Session: 8th and 9th September, 1964" Government Printer, Zomba (1967). Kamuzu Banda's Speech: pp. 10–16. Rose Chibambo's speech: pp. 24–26.

15 Leaving Familiar Spaces (1964–1965)
[i] Johann Alexander Müller, "*The inevitable pipeline into exile*": *Botswana's Role in the Namibian Liberation Struggle* (Basel: Basler Afrika Bibliograpien 2012), p. 227.
[ii] Colin Baker, *Revolt of the Ministers: The Malawi Cabinet Crisis, 1964–1965*. London and New York: I.B. Tauris Publishers (2001), p. 283.
[iii] Letter from Kamuzu Banda to Kenneth Kaunda, 28th November, 1967. Banda Archives, http://webapp1.dlib.indiana.edu/metsnav/africanstudies/navigate.do?oid=http://fedora.dlib.indiana.edu/fedora/get/iudl:869304/METADATA accessed 1 August 2019.

16 Life Away from Home (1965–1994)
[i] Interview with Mrs Barbara Khataza Mlenje, Blantyre, 5 January 2013.

17 The Return (1994)
[i] John Lloyd Lwanda, Kamuzu Banda of Malawi: A Study in Promise, Power and Legacy(Malawi Under Dr Banda 1961–1994), Zomba, Kachere Series: 2009 (first published by Dudu Nsomba Publications, 1993), p. 408.
[ii] Julius Ihonvebere, "Dictatorship, Political Liberalization and Democratization in Malawi," in *Political Liberalization and Democratization in Africa: Lessons from Country Experiences*, eds. Julius Ihonvebere and John Mukum Mbaku (Westport, Praeger Publishers: 2003), p. 244.
[iii] Ibid.
[iv] Ibid.

NOTES

[v] John Lloyd Lwanda, *Kamuzu Banda*, pp. 418–419.

[vi] Maura Mitchell, "'Living Our Faith': the Lenten Pastoral Letter of the Bishops of Malawi and the Shift to Multiparty Democracy 1992–1993," *Journal for the Scientific Study of Religion* 41, no. 5 (2002): 5–18 (p. 6).

[vii] Tania Ghanem, "When Forced Migrants Return 'Home': The Psychosocial Difficulties Returnees Encounter in the Reintegration Process," *RSW Working Paper* No. 16, University of Oxford, Refugee Studies Centre (2003): 1–59 (p. 40).

19 Returning to Old Routes

[i] Colin Baker, *Revolt of the Ministers: The Malawi Cabinet Crisis* (London: IB Tauris, 2001), pp. 71–72.

Photo Credits

The hyperlinks below were active links at the time of publication. The Malawi National Records and Archives Services was called The National Archives of Malawi, when Michael Mutisunge Etter-Phoya (credited as Michaelphoya), assisted in part by staff of both the Archives and the Society, uploaded the photos to Wikimedia Commons on 23 July and 25 August 2014 respectively.

Chibambo's paternal ancestors, the Ngoni, 1911
Society of Malawi, Historical and Scientific, CC BY-SA 4.0,
https://commons.wikimedia.org/w/index.php?curid=34927359

Women pounding maize, undated
Society of Malawi, Historical and Scientific, CC BY-SA 4.0,
https://commons.wikimedia.org/w/index.php?curid=34928111

Wedding of Lewis and Grace Bandawe at St. Michaels Church, 31 May 1913
Society of Malawi, Historical and Scientific, CC BY-SA 4.0,
https://commons.wikimedia.org/w/index.php?curid=34934070

Malawian village, ca. 1960
Society of Malawi, Historical and Scientific, CC BY-SA 4.0,
https://commons.wikimedia.org/w/index.php?curid=34933402

Portrait of Rose Chibambo, 1963
© The Rose L Chibambo Trust

Rose and Edwin Chibambo, 1964
© The Rose L Chibambo Trust

Dr Hastings Kamuzu Banda returns to Nyasaland, 1958
Malawi National Records & Archives Services, CC BY-SA 4.0,
https://commons.wikimedia.org/w/index.php?curid=34386369

Banda as leader of the Nyasaland African Congress campaigning for the end of the Federation, 1958/59
Malawi National Records & Archives Services

Self-government legislative assembly, ca. 1961
Malawi National Records & Archives Services, CC BY-SA 4.0,
https://commons.wikimedia.org/w/index.php?curid=34386369

PHOTO CREDITS

Malawi Party Election Candidates, 15 March 1964
Malawi National Records & Archives Services, CC BY-SA 4.0,
https://commons.wikimedia.org/w/index.php?curid=38666933

The aftermath of the Cabinet Crisis, possibly late 1964
Malawi National Records & Archives Services, CC BY-SA 4.0,
https://commons.wikimedia.org/w/index.php?curid=38667529

Led by a Ngoni praise singer, Banda after being made Life President of Malawi, 1971
Malawi National Records & Archives Services, CC BY-SA 4.0,
https://commons.wikimedia.org/w/index.php?curid=38667322

Chibambo Family Portrait, Malawi, late 1963 or early 1964
© The Rose L Chibambo Trust

Chibambo Family Portrait, Zambia, January 1968
© The Rose L Chibambo Trust

Old Parliament Building, Zomba
Malawi National Records & Archives Services, CC BY-SA 4.0,
https://commons.wikimedia.org/w/index.php?curid=38667494

Portrait of Rose Chibambo on the money
Courtesy of Numis Collection
https://www.numiscollection.com/malawi-200-kwacha-2016-rose-lomathinda-chibambo-a9623-en.html
(slightly modified and used without permission)

Portrait of Rose Chibambo in later life, 15 September 2005
© The Rose L Chibambo Trust

Index

Africanisation 58, 142
African National Congress 102, 156
Armitage, Robert 102, 104, 121, 122
Army, Amazon 129

Banda, Aleke 141, 190
Banda, Hastings Kamuzu 58, 78, 94, 99, 102–105, 109, 120–122, 128–131, 137–148, 153, 156, 166, 171,173–174, 181, 188, 190
Banda, TDT 100–105, 189
Blantyre Secondary School 65, 67
Bwanausi, Augustine 58, 130–131, 140–145, 156, 162, 190
Bwanausi, Ceciwa 120

Cameron, Colin 130–131
Chavura, Violet 120, 187–188, 192, 194
Chibambo, Edwin 3, 8, 19, 65, 71, 76, 77–78, 85, 87, 90, 100, 113–115, 119, 122, 128, 147, 153–155, 161–162, 185, 188
Chibambo, Qabaniso 88, 95, 99, 119, 154, 161, 166
Chibambo, Rose 3, 6, 8, 10, 19, 58, 68, 70, 79, 95, 104, 109, 115, 121–122, 131, 135, 140, 142, 145–148, 156, 165, 171, 174, 181, 195–196, 202
Chibambo, Mrs (NyaPhiri) 88
Chihana, Chakufwa 171
Chikowi, Chief 86, 94–95
Chinyama, James 91, 100, 104
Chipembere, Masauko 100–105, 109, 120, 127, 131, 189–90
Chirwa, Manoah 91, 99–102, 104,
Chirwa, Orton Ching'oli 58, 120, 130, 140, 142, 145, 153, 156, 191
Chirwa, Vera 118, 120, 130, 187, 188–189
Chiume, Kanyama 58, 100–102, 104–105, 109, 122, 130, 131, 140, 142, 145, 153, 156, 189, 190
Chisiza, Dunduzu 101–102, 104, 109, 120, 122, 127, 130, 132, 189
Chisiza, Yatuta 58, 101–102, 120, 128–129, 131, 140, 142, 145, 156, 163, 189, 190
Chokani, Willie 58, 131, 140, 141, 156, 162

Devlin
- Commission 121
- Patrick 117, 118, 121
- Report 121

Ekwendeni 7, 51–52, 57, 59, 65, 69, 75, 118–119, 165
Ephandeni 7

Federation 85–87, 89–90, 92, 94–95, 99, 102–103, 120, 122, 130, 143, 156, 181
Foot, Dingle 117

Gondwe, Goodall 56
Gondwe, Kadonanga 56
Gondwe, Tijepani 119, 187

Haraba, Elizabeth 7, 10

Incwala 11

Kadzamira, Cecilia 117, 128–129, 142

INDEX

Kafukule 7, 51, 52, 69, 165, 166, 194
Kanjedza Detention Camp 119
Kanyanya, Adamson 139
Kaunda, Kenneth 156, 163, 173
Khondowe 7
Khonje, Shadreck 120
KuChawe Manifesto 142
Kumbikano, Clement 94, 99, 104
Kumwenda, Eritas 54

Lenten Letter 174
Livingstonia 7, 19, 54, 59–60, 65, 70, 77, 90, 191

Malawi Congress Party 120, 127, 130, 140, 142–143, 171, 173, 188
Malawi Young Pioneers 153
McAdam, Albert 114, 118
McAdam, Jenny 115, 118
Mkandawire, Mikeka, 91, 100, 104, 130, 189
M'mbelwa II 181
Mthambala, Augustine 120
Mwase, Elizabeth 128, 129
Mzaza, Jessie and Maureen 166–167

Ngwira, McDonald 115–116
Nkumbula, Harry 94, 102
Nyasaland African Congress 88, 90–91, 94, 104–105, 109, 110, 121, 122, 130, 143, 181, 187–188
Nyasulu, Aleck 139, 147
Nyoni, Katola 102

Ramsey Hall 101, 102, 109
Rubadiri
- Gertrude 118
- family 194

Sangala, James 91, 100, 104, 181
Skinner
- James 143
- Report 58, 138, 142, 143, 144
Smith, Catherine 89, 118
Soko, Boston 7, 11
State of Emergency 76, 109, 119, 121–122, 128–129, 130, 146, 163, 189–190

Thangata 120

Walker, Betty 52
Welensky, Roy 78, 92, 94, 121, 127, 129, 143
Women's League 88–93, 100, 118, 120, 122, 127–131, 181, 185–188

Youens, Peter 140, 144, 153
Youth League 58, 189

Ziba, Aaron 7, 19